The Love Letters of Henry VIII to Anne Boleyn

&

Other Correspondence & Documents Concerning the King and His Wives

Henry VIII's first interview with Anne Boleyn

The Love Letters of Henry VIII to Anne Boleyn & Other Correspondence & Documents Concerning the King and His Wives

Henry VIII

and

Henry Ellis

LEONAUR

The Love Letters of Henry VIII to Anne Boleyn
&
Other Correspondence & Documents Concerning the King and His Wives
by Henry VIII
and
Henry Ellis

First published under the title
The Love Letters of Henry VIII to Anne Boleyn
and
Original Letters, Illustrative of English History, Volumes 1 & 2

Leonaur is an imprint
of Oakpast Ltd

Copyright in this form © 2011 Oakpast Ltd

ISBN: 978-0-85706-609-1 (hardcover)
ISBN: 978-0-85706-610-7 (softcover)

http://www.leonaur.com

Contents

How calm and quiet is it, alone
To read and meditate and write,
By none offended and offending none.
(Charles Cotton 1630-87)

Original Introduction

As these letters, with a few reflections on them, may give those that have not leisure to turn over large volumes, just notions of the grounds of King Henry the Eighth's divorce, and arm them against the calumnies of the papists on that subject, I shall give you a faithful copy of them from the originals, now preserved in the Vatican library where they are usually shewn to all strangers, and a true translation of those that were written in French, introducing them with a short view of the most remarkable transactions which preceded, and gave occasion to them. To which end, it may first be observed that, in King Henry the Seventh's time, his eldest son, Prince Arthur, being past fifteen years of age, was married to the Princess Katherine of Spain, who was elder than himself; that they lived together as man and wife for several months, and then, Prince Arthur dying, it was resolved, for reasons of state, that Prince Henry should marry his brother's widow.

This was opposed by Warham, archbishop of Canterbury, as absolutely unlawful, but advised by Fox, bishop of Winchester, who thought all difficulties would be removed by a dispensation, from Rome; accordingly a bull was obtained to that effect, and they were married, the prince being yet under age. But Warham had so possessed the king with scruples against this marriage, that, the day on which the prince was of age, he, by his father's order, protested against it, as null and void; and Henry the Seventh, with his dying breath, persisted in charging his son to break it off intirely.

However, when Henry the Eighth came to the crown, it was resolved in council, that he should renew his marriage; which was done publickly, and he had several children by the queen, who all died young, except the Lady Mary.

After this there appeared no farther disquiet in the king's mind, nor any sign of an intended divorce, till the year 1524, when Cardinal Wolsey, by his legantine mandate, published a bull of the pope's against those that contracted marriage within the forbidden degrees. This mandate is yet extant in the register of Fisher, bishop of Rochester. What followed makes this justly suspected to have been done, on the king's account. To confirm which suspicion, there is a concurring circumstance, in a letter from Simon Grineus to Brucer, dated September 10, 1531, where he says, the king had declared to him, that he had abstained from Queen Katherine, for seven years, upon scruples of conscience.

However, though the king had scruples at that time, yet he concealed them carefully from the world for some years; and the immediate occasion of their breaking out seems to have been given by the French ambassadors, who came to England to treat of several matters, and particularly of a marriage between the Princess Mary and the French king, or the duke of Orleans, his second son. This alternative was at last agreed, though it remained sometime in suspense, because the president of the parliament of Paris doubted, whether the marriage between the king and her mother, being his brother's wife, were good or no.

The bishop of Tarbe made the same objection, and renewed it to the king's ambassadors in France, as appears by King Henry's speech to the mayor and citizens of London, concerning his scruples, where he says, When our ambassadors were last in France and motion was made that the duke of Orleans should marry our said daughter, one of the chief counsellors to the French king said, It were well done to know whether she be the king of England's lawful daughter, or not; for well known it is, that he begat her on his brother's wife, which is directly contrary to God's law, and his precept. That this counsellor was the Bishop of Tarbe, is affirmed by the bishop of Bayonne, in the account he gives of this speech to the court of France, in a letter dated the 27th of November, 1528; yet this very bishop of Tarbe was afterwards advanced to be a cardinal, and was so far from retracting his opinion, that, when he was cardinal of Grandemont, in a letter dated the 27th of March, 1530, he writes to the French court,.

That he had served the Lord Rochford (Anne Boleyn's father) all he could, and that the pope had three several times said to him in secret, that he wished the marriage had been already made in England, either by the legate's dispensation, or otherwise; provided it was not done by him, nor in diminution of his authority, under pretence of the laws of God. The conduct shews, that it was not religion, but political views, that turned the court of Rome against the king's cause, which they at first plainly favoured.

And, now as to the arguments by which the king fortified himself in these scruples. These, as he himself owned, were, that he found by the law of Moses, if a man took his brother's wife, they should die childless; this made him reflect on the death of his children, which he now looked on as a curse from God, for that unlawful marriage. He found Thomas Aquinas (whom he chiefly valued of all the casuists) of opinion, That the laws of Leviticus, about the forbidden degrees of marriage, were moral and eternal, such as obliged all Christians; and that the pope could only dispense with the laws of the church, but not with the laws of God; and when the validity of the marriage came afterwards to be thoroughly canvassed, it appeared that the whole tradition of the church and the opinions of its doctors were against the marriage.

In the year 1527, before Cardinal Wolsey's journey to France, which he began on the 3rd of July, to promote the King's marriage with the duchess of Alenson, the king's scruples were become publick, as two writers testify almost in the same words: This season, says Hall, began a fame in London, that the king's confessor, the bishop of Lincoln, called Dr. Langland, and divers other great clerks, had told the king, that the marriage between him and the Lady Katherine, late wife to his brother, Prince Arthur, was not good, but damnable.

And this suspicion, of the cardinal's going to promote a second match in France, is confirmed by a letter of his, dated Feversham, July the 5th, 1527, where he says, Archbishop Warham had warned him of the great jealousies which Queen Katherine had of his journey. And by another letter, dated August the 1st, 1527, where he labours to satisfy the king, that the pope's dispensation was in itself null and void. All these particulars will be the stronger proofs of the cardinal's intention, when it shall be proved that the cardinal could then have no thoughts of Anne Boleyn, whose father, the Lord Rochford, came over to England from France with the duchess of Alenson's picture to shew it to King Henry; and it was then, in all probability, that Anne Boleyn came over with him; for, though she had been in England in 1522, yet she did not stay long but returned into the service of Claude, queen of France, where she continued till that queen died, which was in 1524, and then went into the duchess of Alenson's service, which she left probably at this time.

Soon after her coming into England, she was taken into Queen Katherine's court, where the Lord Piercy courted her, and was upon the point of marrying her had not Cardinal Wolsey, by the king's order, prevented it; and, as the same author assures us, it was not till after the cardinal's return from France, which was on the last day of September, 1527, that the king opened his affection for Anne Boleyn to him.

Why then do the papists pretend to say, that the king would never have had thoughts of a divorce, or scruples against his first marriage, had not his unlawful passion for Mrs. Boleyn prompted him to them? Whereas it is plainly proved that the king's scruples were infused in him from his infancy, on the justest grounds; that they were revived in him three years before they were made public, and that they were commonly talked of, and a new match contrived for him to the duchess of Alenson, before Anne Boleyn appeared at court. All which will still appear more clearly in the ensuing letters.

But, before I make any remarks on these, I must first give a short account of the king's negotiations at Rome, without which some of them cannot be understood. In the end of 1527, the king solicited the pope for a commission to judge the validity of his marriage with Queen Katherine, which after some time was obtained in a bull, dated the 13th of April, 1528, impowering Cardinal Wolsey, with the archbishop, or any other English bishop to judge the marriage. But this was not made use of; perhaps because it was thought that a stranger ought to be employed, that the proceeding might be more impartial. So a new commission was desired, and obtained, bearing date the 6th of June, in which the cardinals Wolsey and Campegio (an Italian) were appointed joint legates to judge the marriage.

And, to make this the surer, there was a pollicitation (or promise) procured on the 23rd of July, 1528, That the pope would never inhibit or revoke this commission to judge the marriage; and a decretal bull, which contained an absolute decision of the cause, which was only shewn to the king, and cardinal Wolsey, by Campegio; but all these precautions which were admitted of, when the pope was in a distressed condition, did not restrain his holiness from sending one Campana before the end of the year, to see the decretal bull secretly burnt; and from recalling the legate's commission, and avocating the cause to Rome the next year, when his affairs were more flourishing, and the emperor (who was Queen Katherine's nephew) had granted all his demands.

Now as to the letters themselves. It may be presumed reasonably, that, if there had been anything in them that had reflected on the king's honour, or on Anne Boleyn's, they would certainly have been published by the papists at that very time; for they were in their hands soon after they were written, as appears from this passage in Lord Herbert's History.

> When Cardinal Campegio came to take ship, the searchers, upon pretence he carried either money or letters from England to Rome, ransacked all his coffers, bags, and pa-

pers, not without hope, certainly to recover that decretal bull our king so much longed for. I find also (some relation) that divers love-letters between our king and Mistress Boleyn, being conveyed out of the king's cabinet, were sought for, though in vain; they having been formerly sent to Rome.

To explain this account, it must be supposed, that they were taken, not out of the king's, but out of Anne Boleyn's cabinet; this is the more probable, because, in fact, they are all letters from the king to her; whereas, if his cabinet had been rifled, her answers to him would have been more likely to be found there.

As to the time in which the king's letters to Anne Boleyn were written, in all probability, it was immediately after her dismission from the court, which was done to silence the clamours of the people on her account; but she was sent away in so abrupt a manner, that she determined to absent herself altogether; which made the king soon repent of his severity, and press her to come back; but this was not obtained for a long time, nor without great difficulty; as appears by some of the following letters.

The time of her dismission was not till May, 1528, for there is a letter extant from Fox to Gardiner, at Rome, dated London, May the 4th, 1528, where he writes, of his landing at Sandwich, May the 2nd,—His coming that night to Greenwich, where the king lay,—His being commanded to go to Mistress Anne's chamber in the Tilt-yard—And declaring to her their expedition in the king's cause, and their hastening the coming of the legate—To her great rejoicing and comfort—Then came the king, to whom he delivered his letters,—and opened his negotiations—Then he went to the cardinal, etc.

Soon after the date of this letter she was dismissed; for, in the first of the letters that follow, the king makes excuses for the necessity of their being asunder; and, in the second complains of her unwillingness to return to court. In neither of these is a word of the sweating sickness, which raged violently in June; and of which he speaks in his third letter, as of a thing that had lasted some time, and, of which, he had formed many observations from experience. Between this letter, which seems to have been writ in July, and the sixth, which, mentioning the legates arrival at Paris must have been written in the end of September, there are two letters, which by the earnestness of the business, were plainly written within a few days of one another.

Probably, soon after the latter of these were sent by the king, where he expressed how much he was pleased with her answer to his earnest desire in the former, in the heat of his gratitude, he paid a visit to his mistress, in which time they wrote a joint letter to Cardinal Wolsey, which is added in the appendix, where the king expresses his wonder, that he has not yet heard of the legate Campegio's arrival at Paris; which makes it probable this happened in September. The king stayed not long with her after this; for, when she had received the cardinal's answer, she writes a second letter, without mentioning the king's being there; and, again shews impatience to hear of the legate's coming, of which, the king gave her the first news soon after.

But, to return to the fourth letter, which from all these particulars may be supposed to have been written in August; it is the most important in all the collection, for it fixes the time when his affection to Anne Boleyn began. He complains in it, That he had been above a whole year struck with the dart of love, and not yet sure whether he shall fail, or find a place in her heart or affection.

Now, by the nature of his complaint, it is visible, that he pleads all the merits that a long attendance could give him, and, therefore, if, instead of a year, he should have called it a year and a half, or two years, he would certainly have done it to make his argument the stronger. It may likewise be probably concluded from the same words, that he had not then known her much above half a year; for it would have been an ill compliment in him, to let her understand that he had seen her some time, before he was at all in love with her.

These remarks confirm the account already given, of her coming from France with her father, and, by that means, serve to establish the king's vindication from the scandal thrown on

15

him by the papists, that he had no scruples about his marriage, till he saw Anne Boleyn.

Though it may be here questioned, how the time of any particular letter can be known, since they have no date, and therefore may have been put out of their order. But those, that will read them with any attention, will find a chain of circumstances referred to that plainly show they were laid together by one that knew the order in which they were written, very likely by Anne Boleyn herself; and whoever stole them, as he took them all together, so would be careful no doubt, to keep them in the order he found them in, that the discoveries to be made from them might be the more complete.

It will not be doubted by any that read these letters, that the king's affection to Anne Boleyn was altogether upon honourable terms. There appears no pretension to any favours, but when the legates shall have paved the way. There is but one offence that can be taken at these letters, which is, that there are indecent expressions in them. But this is to be imputed to the simplicity and unpoliteness of that age which allowed too great liberties of that sort; and it must be owned by his enemies, that there are but three or four of these sallies in all the collection, and that there are letters that make much more for the king's piety and virtue, than those irregularities can sully his character.

In the fifth letter he tells her, God can do it, if he pleases; to whom I pray once a day for that end, and hope, that, at length, my prayers will be heard.

In the sixth, I trust shortly to enjoy, what I have so longed for, to God's pleasure, and our both comforts.

In the ninth, praying God, that (and it be His pleasure), to send us shortly togydder. Surely these religious expressions would have been very improper, to make an unlawful passion succeed.

In the thirteenth, speaking of the ill character of one that was proposed to be made abbess of Wilton, he writes, I would not, for all the gold in the world, clog your conscience nor mine, to make her ruler of a house which is of so ungodly demeanour;

nor I trust you would not, that, neither for brother nor sister, I should so destrain mine honour or conscience. The whole letter is of an excellent strain, and would have been a very improper exhortation to one against whose virtue he had a design.

The last of the letters mentions the legate's illness as a reason why he had not yet entered upon his office; which shews that the correspondence ended at least in May 1529 when the process began.

There is but one thing after the letters, that it seems very material to add here in the king's defence and that is, the approbation of his cause by the learned men of Europe.

During the trial, Warham and Fisher, who were the advocates for the queen, declared, That they having been lately consulted by the king, etc., had answered, that the king's conscience was disturbed and shaken, not without the weightiest and strongest reasons.

After the legates had trifled some months, and at last, Campegio, under a pretence of the rules of the court of Rome, had adjourned the court for three months; during which time he obtained an avocation from the pope; the king was advised by Cranmer, not to depend longer on the decisions of the see of Rome, but to consult the several universities of Europe, as well as his own, about the validity of his marriage.

One Crook was employed in this negotiation, and he obtained the opinion of almost all the universities whither he went, for the nullity of the marriage; yet he complains in his letters that he was in great straits from the small allowance he had. And, in an original bill of his accounts it appears that he never gave above a few crowns to any that writ on the king's side; whereas the emperor gave a benefice of five hundred *ducates* to one, and of six hundred crowns to another, that writ for the queen. Yet, though on the one side men were poorly paid for their trouble, and on the other richly rewarded, yet the most eminent men were universally for the king.

It may here be added that Erasmus, whose name was in the greatest esteem at that time, though he could not be prevailed with to write for the king, for fear of the pope and the emperor, in whose dominions he lived; yet he went so far as to give great encomiums of the worth and virtues of Sir Thomas Boleyn, then earl of Wiltshire in his book, *De Preparatione ad Mortem*, which he dedicates to him; and this was all the approbation that his circumstances made it convenient for him to shew of the king's cause.

On this general consent of the learned in his favour, the king was told he might proceed to a second marriage, the first being of itself null and void; and, accordingly, he married Anne Boleyn, the twenty-fifth of January, 1533.

The Letters of King Henry VIII
to Anne Boleyn

KING HENRY THE EIGHTH

Letter 1

My mistress and friend, I and my heart put ourselves in your hands, begging you to recommend us to your favour, and not to let absence lessen your affection to us. For it were a great pity to increase our pain, which absence alone does sufficiently, and more than I could ever have thought; bringing to my mind a point of astronomy, which is, that the farther the moors are from us, the farther too is the sun, and yet his heat is the more scorching; so it is with our love, we are at a distance from one another, and yet it keeps its fervency, at least on my side. I hope the like on your part, assuring you that the uneasiness of absence is already too severe for me; and when I think of the continuance of that which I must of necessity suffer, it would seem intolerable to me, were it not for the firm hope I have of your unchangeable affection for me; and now, to put you sometimes in mind of it, and seeing I cannot be present in person with you, I send you the nearest thing to that possible, that is, my picture set in bracelets, with the whole device, which you know already, wishing myself in their place, when it shall please you. This from the hand of

Your servant and friend H. Rex

LETTER 2

Because the time seems to me very long, since I have heard from you, or concerning your health; the great affection I have for you has obliged me to send this bearer to be better informed, both of your health and pleasure, particularly because, since my last parting with you, I have been told, that you have intirely changed the opinion in which I left you, and that you would neither come to court with your mother, nor any other way; which report, if true, I cannot enough wonder at, being persuaded in my own mind, that I have never committed any offence against you; and it seems a very small return for the great love I bear you, to be kept at a distance from the person and presence of a woman in the world that I value the most; and, if you love me with as much affection as I hope you do, I am sure, the distance of our two persons would be a little uneasy to you. Though this does not belong so much to the mistress as the servant. Consider well, my mistress, how greatly your absence grieves me; I hope it is not your will that it should be so; but, if I heard for certain, that you yourself desired it, I could do no other than complain of my ill fortune, and by degrees abate my great folly; and so, for want of time, I make an end of my rude letter, desiring you to give credit to this bearer in all he will tell you from me. Written by the hand of your intire servant.

LETTER 3

The uneasiness, my doubts about your health gave me, disturbed and frightened me extremely, and I should not have had any quiet without hearing a certain account. But now since you have yet felt nothing, I hope it is with you as with us; for when we were at Walton, two ushers, two *valets de chambre*, and your brother, master-treasurer, fell ill, and are now quite well; and since we have returned to your house at Hondson, we have been perfectly well, God be praised, and have not, at present, one sick person in the family; and, I think, if you would retire from the Surrey side, as we did, you would escape all danger.

There is another thing that may comfort you, which is, that in truth in this distemper few or no women have been taken ill, and besides, no person of our court, and few elsewhere have died of it. For which reasons I beg of you, my intirely beloved, not to frighten yourself, nor to be too uneasy at our absence. For, wherever I am, I am yours, and yet we must sometimes submit to our misfortunes, for, whoever will struggle against fate, is generally but so much the farther from gaining his end; wherefore, comfort yourself, and take courage, and make this misfortune as easy to you as you can, and I hope shortly to make you sing for joy of your recall. No more at present for lack of time, but that I wish you in my arms, that I might a little dispel your unreasonable thoughts. Written by the hand of him, who is, and always will be yours.

My, H. Rex, Lovely

LETTER 4

By turning over in my thoughts the contents of your last letters, I have put myself into a great agony, not knowing how to understand them, whether to my disadvantage as I understand them, whether to my disadvantage as I understood some others, or not; I beseech you now, with the greatest earnestness, to let me know your whole intention, as to the love between us two. For I must of necessity obtain this answer of you, having been above a whole year struck with the dart of love, and not yet sure whether I shall fail, or find a place in your heart and affection.

This uncertainty has hindered me of late from naming you my mistress, since you only love me with an ordinary affection; but if you please to do the duty of a true and loyal mistress, and to give up yourself, body and heart, to me, who will be, as I have been your most loyal servant (if your rigour does not forbid me) I promise you that not only the name shall be given you, but also that I will take you for my mistress, casting off all others that are in competition with you, out of my thoughts and affection, and serving you only.

I beg you to give an intire answer to this my rude letter, that I may know on what and how far I may depend. But, if it does not please you to answer me in writing, let me know some place, where I may have it by word of mouth, and I will go thither with all my heart. No more for fear of tiring you. Written by the hand of him, who would willingly remain yours.   H. Rex

LETTER 5

For a present so valuable that nothing could be more (considering the whole of it) I return you my most hearty thanks, not only on account of the costly diamond, and the ship in which the solitary damsel is tossed about; but chiefly for the fine interpretation and too humble submission which your goodness hath made to me. For I think it would be very difficult for me to find an occasion to deserve it, if I was not afflicted by your great humanity and favour, which I have sought, do seek, and will always seek to preserve by all the services in my power; and this is my firm intention and hope, according to the motto, *Aut illic aut nullibi* (either there or nowhere).

The demonstrations of your affection are such, the fine thoughts of your letter so cordially expressed that they oblige me forever to honour, love and serve you sincerely, beseeching you to continue in the same firm and constant purpose; and assuring you, that, on my part, I will not only make you a suitable return, but out-do you in loyalty of heart if it be possible.

I desire you also, that, if at any time before this I have in any sort offended you, you would give me the same absolution which you ask, assuring you, that hereafter my heart shall be dedicated to you alone. I wish my body was so too; God can do it, if he pleases; to whom I pray once a day for that end; hoping that at length my prayers will be heard.

I wish the time may be short, but I shall think it long, till

we shall see one another. Written by the hand of the secretary, who in heart, body, and will, is

Your loyal and most assured servant

H. autre 🖤 ne cherce **R.**

(The signature means "H. seeks no other (heart). R.")

Letter 6

The reasonable request of your last letter, with the pleasure I also take to know them, causes me to send you now this news. The legat, which we most desire, arrived at Paris on Sunday or Monday last past; so that I trust, by the next Monday, to hear of his arrival at Calais: and then, I trust, within a while after, to enjoy that which I have so longed for, to God's pleasure, and our both comforts. No more to you, at this present, mine awne darling, for lake of time; but that I would you were in myne arms, or I in yours; for I think it long since I kyset you. Written after the killing of an hart, at XI of the clock; minding with God's grace tomorrow, mightily tymely to kill another, by the hand of him, which I trust shortly shall be yours.

Henry R.

LETTER 7

Darling, though I have scant leisure, yet, remembering my promise, I thought it convenient to certify you breevly, in what case our affairs stand. As touching a lodging for you, we have gotten wone, by my lord cardinal's means, the like whereof could not have been found hereabouts for all causes, as this bearer shall more shew you. At touching our other affairs, I ensure you there can be no more done, or more diligence used, nor all manner of dangers better both foreseen and provided for, so that I trust it shall be hereafter to both our comforts, the specialities whereof were both too long to be writtne, and hardly by messenger to be declared. Wherefore till you repair hydder, I keep something in store, trusting it shall not be long to. For I have caused my lord, your father to make his provisions with speed. And thus, for lake of tyme, darling, I make an end of my letter, writeing with the hand of him, which I would were yours.

H.R.

LETTER 8

Though it does not belong to a gentleman to take his lady in the place of servant, however, in following your desires, I willingly grant it, so that you may be more agreeably in the place that you yourself have chosen, than you have been in that which I gave you. I shall be heartily obliged to you, if you please to have some remembrance of me. 6. N. R. 1. de R. O. M.V. E. Z.   Henry Rex

LETTER 9

The cause of my writeing at this time (good sweetheart) is wonly to understand off your good health and prosperity, whereof to know I would be as glad in manner myne awne, praying God, that and it be his pleasure, to send us shortly togydder, for I promise you I long for it, howbeit, trust it shall not be long too; and seeing my darling is absent, I can no less do, than to send her some flesh representing my name, which is hart's fleshe for Henry, prognosticating, that hereafter, God willing, you must enjoy some of mine, which if he pleased I wolde were now.

As touching your sister's matter, I have caused Walter Welche to write to my lord mine mind therein, whereby I trust that Eve shall not have power to deceave Adam. For surely, whatsoever is said, it cannot so stand with his honour, but that he must needs take her his natural daughter now in his extream necessity. No more to you at this time, mine own darling, but that with a wishe I would we were togydder one evening with the hand your   H. R.

LETTER 10

Although, my mistress, you have not been pleased to remember the promise which you made me when I was last with you which was, that I should hear news of you, and have an answer to my last letter; yet I think it belongs to a true servant (since otherwise he can know nothing) to send to enquire of his mistress's health; and, for to acquit myself of the office of a true servant, I send you this letter begging you to give me an account of the state you are in, which I pray God may continue as long in prosperity, as I with my own; and, that you may the oftener remember me, I send you by this bearer, a buck killed late last night by my hand, hoping, when you eat of it, you will think on the hunter; and thus for want of more room I will make an end of my letter. Written by the hand of your servant, who often wishes you in your brother's room.

H. Rex

LETTER 11

The approach of the time, which I have so long expected, rejoices me so much, that it seems almost ready come. However, the entire accomplishment cannot be till the two persons meet, which meeting is more desired by me than anything in this world; for what joy can be greater upon earth, than to have the company of her who is my dearest friend? Knowing likewise that she does the same on her part, the thinking on which gives great pleasure. You may judge what an effect the presence of that person must have on me, whose absence has made a greater wound in my heart than either words or writing can express, and which nothing can cure, but her return; I beg you, dear mistress, to tell your father from me, that I desire him to hasten the appointment by two days, that he may be in court before the old term, or at farthest on the day prefixed; for otherwise I shall think, he will not do the lover's turn, as he said he would, nor answer my expectation. No more at present, for want of time; hoping shortly by word of mouth I shall tell you the rest of my sufferings from your absence. Written by the hand of the secretary, who wishes himself at present privately with you, and who is, and always will be,

Your royal and most assured servant

H. no other (AB) seeks Rex

LETTER 12

There came to me in the night the most afflicting news possible. For I have reason to grieve upon three accounts. First, because I heard of the sickness of my mistress, whom I esteem more than all the world, whose health I desire as much as my own, and the half of whose sickness I would willingly bear to have her cured. Secondly, because I fear I shall suffer yet longer that tedious absence which has hitherto given me all possible uneasiness, and, as far as I can judge, is like to give me more. I pray God he would deliver me from so troublesome a tormentor. The third reason is, because the physician, in whom I trust most, is absent at present, when he could do me the greatest pleasure.

For I should hope by him, and his means to obtain one of my principal joys in this world, that is, my mistress cured; however, in default of him, I send you the second, and the only one left, praying God that he may soon make you well, and then I shall love him more than ever. I beseech you to be governed by his advices with relation to your illness; by your doing which I hope shortly to see you again, which will be to me a greater cordial than all the precious stones in the world. Written by the secretary who is, and always will be

Your loyal and most assured servant

H.(AB) R.

LETTER 13

Since your last letters, myne awne darling, Walter Welche,
Master Brown, John Carre, Yrion of Brearton, John Cocke,
the pothecary, be fallen of the swett in this house, and
thenkyed be God all well recovered, so that as yet the
plague is not fully ceased here; but I trust shortly it shall
by the mercy of God; the rest of us yet be well, and I trust
shall pass it, either not to have it, or at least as easily as the
rest have don. As touching the matter of Wylton, my lord
cardinal hath had the nunys before him, and examined
them, Master Bell being present, which hath certified me
that for a truth, that she hath confessed herself (which
we would have had abbesse) to have had two children by
two sundry priests: and, furder since hath been keeped by
a servant of the Lord Broke, that was, and that not long
ago.

Wherefore I would not for all the world clog your conscience nor mine to make her ruler of a house which is
of so ungodly demeanour; nor I trust you would not, that
neither for brother nor sister I should so destain my honour or conscience; and as touching the pryoress, or Dame
Ellenor's eldest sister, though there is not any evident case
proved against them, and that the pryoresse is so old, that
of many years she could not be as she was named; yet
notwithstanding, to do you pleasure, I have done that neither of them shall have it, but that some other and good
and well disposed woman shall have it; whereby the house
shall be the better reformed (whereof, I ensure you, it had

much need) and God much the better served; as touching abode at Hever, do therein as best shall you like; for
you know best what aire doth best for you; but I would
it were come thereto (if it pleased God) that neither of us
need care for that, for I ensure you I think it long. Suche is
fallen sick of the swett, and ther for I send you this bearer,
because I think you long to hear tydings from us, as we do
in likewise from you. Writeing with the hand

Devotre seul

H.R.

LETTER 14

Darling, these shall be only to advertise you, that this bearer and his fellow, be dispatched with as many things to compass our matter, and to bring it to pass as our wits could imagine or devise, which brought to pass, as I trust by their diligence, it shall be, shortly you and I shall have our desired end, which should be more to my heart's ease, and more quietness to my minde, than any other thing in this world, as with God's Grace shortly I trust shall be proved, but not so soon as I would it were, yet I will assure you there shall be no tyme lost that may be won, and further cannot be done, for *ultra posse non est esse*: keep him not too long with you, but desire him for your sake to make the more speed, for, the sooner we shall have word from him, the sooner shall our matter come to pass; and thus, upon trust of your short repair to London, I make an end of my letter, mine awne sweetheart. Writne with the hand of him which desireth as much to be yours, as you do to have him. H. R.

LETTER 15

Darling, I heartily recommend me to you, assertaining you, that I am not a little perplexed with such things as your brother shall on my part declare unto you, to whom I pray you give full credence, for it were too long to write. In my last letters I writ to you that I trusted shortly to see you, which is better known at London than with any that is about me, whereof I not a little mervelle but lake of discreet handling must needs be the cause thereof. No more to you at this time, but that I trust shortly, our meeting shall not depend upon other men's light handlings but upon your awne. Writne with the hand of him that longeth to be yours. H. R.

LETTER 16

Myne awne sweetheart, this shall be to advertise you of the great ellingness that I find here since your departing, for I assure you, methinketh the tyme longer since your departing now last then I was wont to do a whole fortnight; I think your kindness and my fervence of love causeth it, for otherwise I would not thought it possible, that for so little a while it should have grieved me, but now that I am coming towards you, methinketh my pains been half released, and also I am right well comforted, insomuch that my book maketh substantially for my matter, in writing whereof I have spent above iiii hours this day, which caused me now to write the shorter letter to you at this tyme, because of some payne in my head, wishing myself (especially an evening) in my sweetheart's arms whose pretty duckys I trust shortly to kysse. Writtne with the hand of him that was, is, and shall be yours by his will.

H.R.

LETTER 17

To informe you what joye it is to me to understand of
your conformableness with reason, and of the suppress-
ing of your inutile and vain thoughts and with the bridle
of reasone, I assure you all the good of this world could
not counterpoise for my satisfaction the knowledge and
certainty thereof; wherefor, good sweetheart, continue the
same not only in this, but in all your doings hereafter, for
thereby shall come both to you and me the greatest quiet-
nesse that may be in this world. The cause why this bearer
stayeth so long, is the business that I have had dresse up
geer for you, which I trust ere long to see you occupy, and
then I trust to occupy yours, which shall be recompence
enough to me for all my pains and labours.
The unfayned sicknessof this well-willing legate doth
somewhat retard his accesse to your person, but I trust
veryly, when God shall send him health, he will with diligence recompense his demure, for I know well where he
hath said (lamenting the sayinge, and brute (Noyse) that
he shall be thought imperial) that it shall be well known
in this matter, that he is not imperial. And this for lake of
tyme, farewell. Writtne with the hand which faine would
be yours, and so is the heart.

H. R.

Letters of Anne Boleyn
and Other Documents

ANNE BOLEYN

LETTER FROM ANNE BOLEYN TO KING HENRY VIII
LATE SUMMER 1526
(Believed to be the first love letter written to the King)

Sire,

It belongs only to the august mind of a great king, to whom Nature has given a heart full of generosity towards the sex, to repay by favours so extraordinary an artless and short conversation with a girl. Inexhaustible as is the treasury of your majesty's bounties, I pray you to consider that it cannot be sufficient to your generosity; for, if you recompense so slight a conversation by gifts so great, what will you be able to do for those who are ready to consecrate their entire obedience to your desires?

How great soever may be the bounties I have received, the joy that I feel in being loved by a king whom I adore, and to whom I would with pleasure make a sacrifice of my heart, if fortune had rendered it worthy of being offered to him, will ever be infinitely greater.

The warrant of maid of honour to the queen induces me to think that your majesty has some regard for me, since it gives me means of seeing you oftener, and of assuring you by my own lips (which I shall do on the first opportunity) that I am,

Your majesty's very obliged and very obedient servant, without any reserve,

Anne Bulen[1]

---

1. Variation of her surname as she spelt it in the letter.

Anne Boleyn To Cardinal Wolsey

My lord, in my most humble wise that my heart can think, I desire you to pardon me that I am so bold, to trouble you with my simple and rude writing, esteeming it to proceed from her, that is much desirous to know that your grace does well, as I perceive by this bearer that you do. The which I pray God long to continue, as I am most bound to pray; for I do know the great pains and troubles that you have taken for me, both day and night, is never like to be recompenced on my part, but alonely in loving you, next unto the king's grace, above all creatures living.

And I do not doubt, but the daily proof of my deeds shall manifestly declare and affirm my writing to be true, and I do trust you do think the same. My lord, I do assure you, I do long to hear from you news of the legate; for I do hope, and they come from you, they shall be very good, and I am sure you desire it as much as I, and more, and it were possible, as I know it is not; and thus, remaining in a steadfast hope, I make an end of my letter, written with the hand of her that is most bound to be.

Your humble servant

Anne Boleyn

(Postcript by King Henry)
The writer of this letter would not cease till she had caused me likewise to set to my hand; desiring you, though it be short, to take it in good part. I ensure you, there is neither of us, but that greatly desireth to see you, and much

more joyous to hear that you have escaped this plague so well, and trusting the fury thereof to be passed, especially with them that keepeth good diet, as I trust you do. The not hearing of the legate's arrival in France, causeth us somewhat to muse; notwithstanding, we trust by your diligence and vigilancy (with the assistance of Almighty God) shortly to be eased out of that trouble. No more to you at this time; but that I pray God send you as good health prosperity, as the writer would.

By your loving sovereign and friend

Henry R.

Letter from Anne Boleyn to Cardinal Thomas Wolsey, 1529

My lord,

Though you are a man of great understanding, you cannot avoid being censured by everybody for having drawn on yourself the hatred of a king who had raised you to the highest degree to which the greatest ambition of a man seeking his fortune can aspire. I cannot comprehend, and the king still less, how your reverent lordship, after having allured us by so many fine promises about divorce, can have repented of your purpose, and how you could have done what you have, in order to hinder the consummation of it. What, then, is your mode of proceeding? You quarrelled with the queen to favour me at the time when I was less advanced in the king's good graces; and after having therein given me the strongest marks of your affection, your lordship abandons my interests to embrace those of the queen.

I acknowledge that I have put much confidence in your professions and promises, in which I find myself deceived. But, for the future, I shall rely on nothing by the protection of Heaven and the love of my dear king, which alone will be able to set right again those plans which you have broken and spoiled, and to place me in that happy station which God wills, the king so much wishes, and which will be entirely to the advantage of the kingdom. The wrong you have done me has caused me much sorrow; but I feel infinitely more in seeing myself betrayed by a man who pretended to enter into my interests only to discover the secrets of my heart. I acknowledge that, believing you sincere, I have been too precipitate in my confidence; it is this which has induced, and still induces me, to keep more moderation in avenging myself, not being able to forget that I have been

Your servant,

Anne Boleyn.

King Henry in Queen Anne's name to Lord Cobham

(Announcing the birth of her daughter the word 'prince' was written in the first instance by the confident king, and an 's' added after the queen's delivery, leading to the error for some that Anne Boleyn had brought Henry VIII. a living son, as the feminising 's' was omitted in some copies of the circular.)

To Lord Cobham by the Queen

Right trusty and well beloved, we greet you well. And whereas it hath pleased the goodness of Almighty God, of his infinite mercy and grace, to send, to us, at this time, good speed in the deliverance and bringing forth of a prince*s*, to the great joy, rejoice, and infinite comfort of my lord, us, and all his good subjects of this his realm, for the which his inestimable benevolence, so showed unto us, we have no little cause to give high thanks, laud, and praising our said Maker, like as we do most lowly, humbly, and with all the inward desire of our heart. And inasmuch as we undoubtedly trust, that this our good speed is to you great pleasure, comfort, and consolation, we, therefore, by these our letters advertise you thereof, desiring and heartily praying you to give, with us, unto Almighty God, high thanks, glory, laud, and praising; and to pray for the good health, prosperity, and continual preservation, of the said prince*s* accordingly. Given under our signet, at my lord's manor of Greenwich, the 7th day of September, in the 20th year of my said lord's reign.

---

1. This letter precisely fixes the day of Elizabeth's birth on the 7th of September, 1533; hitherto a point of controversy with historians, who quote either 5th or 13th. The same form of circular served to announce the birth of Edward VI. Princess was always spelt at that era with only one 's'.

Letter of Anne Boleyn to Thomas Cromwell, 1535

Master Secretary, I pray you despatch with speed this matter, for mine honour lies much on it, and what should the king's attorney do with Pointz's obligation, since I have the child by the king's grace's gift, but only to trouble him hereafter, which by no means I will suffer, and thus fare you as well as I would ye did.

    Your loving mistress,

                Anne the Queen.

Thomas Cranmer to King Henry VIII

If it be true what is openly reported of the Queen's grace, if men had a right estimation of things, they should not esteem any part of your grace's honour to be touched thereby, but her honour only to be clearly disparaged. And I am in such perplexity, that my mind is clean amazed, for I never had a better opinion in woman than I had of her, which maketh me think that she should not be culpable. Now I think that your grace best knoweth, that next unto your grace I was most bound unto her of all creatures living. Wherefore I must humbly beseech your grace to suffer me in that which both God's law, nature, and her kindness, bindeth me, unto that I may (with your grace's favour) wish and pray for her.

And from what condition your grace, of your only mere goodness, took her, and set the crown upon her head, I repute him not your grace's faithful servant and subject, nor true to the realm, that would not desire the offence to be without mercy punished, to the example of all others. And as I loved her not a little, for the love I judged her to bear towards God and his holy Gospel, so, if she be proved culpable, there is not one that loveth God and his Gospel that will ever favour her, but they must hate her above all other, and the more they love the Gospel, the more they will hate her, for then there never was creature in our time that so much slandered the Gospel.

And God hath sent her this punishment, for that she feign- edly hath professed the Gospel in her mouth, and not in her heart and deed, and though she hath offended, so that she hath deserved never to be reconciled to your grace's favour, yet God Almighty hath manifoldly declared his goodness towards your grace, and never offended you.

Cranmer added a postscript:

"that the lord-chancellor and others of his majesty's house had sent him to the Star-Chamber, and there declared such things as the king wished him to be shown, which had made him lament that such faults could be proved on the queen as he had heard from their relations."

ANNE BOLEYN TO KING HENRY:
(The last letter)

Sir, Your grace's displeasure, and my imprisonment, are
things so strange unto me, as what to write, or what to
excuse, I am altogether ignorant. Whereas you send unto
me (willing me to confess a truth, and so obtain your favour) by such an one whom you know to be mine antient
professed enemy; I no sooner received this message by
him,[1] than I rightly conceived your meaning; and if, as
you say, confessing a truth indeed may procure my safety,
I shall with all willingness and duty perform your command. But let not your grace ever imagine that your poor
wife will ever be brought to acknowledge a fault, where
not so much as a thought thereof preceded.

And to speak a truth, never prince had wife more loyal in
all duty, and in all true affection, than you have ever found
in Anne Boleyn, with which name and place I could willingly have contented myself, if God and your grace's pleasure had been so pleased. Neither did I at any time so far
forget myself in my exaltation, or received queenship, but
that I always looked for such an alteration as now I find;
for the ground of my preferment being on no surer foun-
dation than your grace's fancy, the least alteration, I knew,

---

1. This enemy had been supposed to be Lady Rochford but the relative *him* cannot
apply to her. It is possible it was the Duke of Suffolk, who always came ostenta-
tiously forward to help to crush any victim henry was sacrificing. he was one of her
judges and pronounced her guilty, and he witnessed her death, being on the scaffold
with no friendly intention.

52

was fit and sufficient to draw that fancy to some other subject. You have chosen me from a low estate to be your queen and companion, far beyond my desert or desire.

If then, you found me worthy of such honour, good your grace let not any light fancy, or bad counsel of mine enemies, withdraw your princely favour from me; neither let that stain, that unworthy stain of a disloyal heart, towards your good grace, ever cast so foul a blot on your most dutiful wife, and the infant princess, your daughter; try me, good king, but let me have a lawful trial, and let not my sworn enemies sit as my accusers and judges; yea, let me receive an open trial, for my truth shall fear no open shame; then shall you see, either mine innocency cleared, your suspicion and conscience satisfied, the ignominy and slander of the world stopped, or my guilt openly declared.

So that, whatsoever God or you may determine of me, your grace may be freed from an open censure; and mine offence being so lawfully proved, your grace is at liberty, both before God and man, not only to execute worthy punishment on me as an unlawful wife, but to follow your affection already settled on that party,[2] for whose sake I am now as I am, whose name I could some good while since have pointed unto; your grace being not ignorant of my suspicion therein.

But, if you have already determined of me, and that not only my death, but an infamous slander must bring you the enjoying of your desired happiness; then I desire of God, that he will pardon your great sin therein, and likewise mine enemies, the instruments thereof; and that he will not call you to a strict account for your unprincely and cruel usage of me, at his general judgment-seat, where both you and myself must shortly appear, and in whose judgment, I doubt not (whatsoever the world may think of me), mine innocence shall be openly known, and suf-

2. Jane Seymour.

ficiently cleared.

My last and only request shall be, that myself may only bear the burthen of your grace's displeasure, and that it may not touch the innocent souls of those poor gentlemen, who, as I understand, are likewise in strait imprisonment for my sake. If ever I have found favour in your sight; if ever the name of Anne Boleyn hath been pleasing in your ears, then let me obtain this request, and I will so leave to trouble your grace any further, with mine earnest prayers to the Trinity to have your grace in his good keeping, and to direct you in all your actions. From my doleful prison in the Tower, this sixth of May.

Your most loyal and ever faithful wife

Anne Boleyn

LORD BACON'S ACCOUNT OF ANNE BOLEYN'S
MEMORANDUM AT THE BOTTOM OF THE LAST LETTER

(The messenger however dare not carry this to the king, Lord Bacon's grandfather Sir Antony Cooke, was tutor to Edward VI., his aunt, Lady Cecil, and his mother, Lady Bacon, both in Queen Mary's service connected with the court of England, he therefore knew when they were uttered, as all these persons must have heard these facts from witnesses.)

Commend me to his majesty, and tell him he hath been ever constant in his career of advancing me; from a private gentlewoman he made me a marchioness, from a marchioness a queen, and now he hath left no higher degree of honour, he gives my innocency the crown of martyrdom.

ANNE BOLEYN'S WORDS AFTER
BEING CONDEMNED TO DEATH

(Clasping her hands and raising her eyes) Oh Father! Oh Creator! Thou who art the way, the life, and the truth, knowest whether I have deserved this death.

(Then turning to her earthly judges, she said,) My lords, I will not say your sentence is unjust, nor presume that my reasons can prevail against your convictions. I am willing to believe that you have sufficient reasons for what you have done, but then they must be other than those which have been produced in court, for I am clear of all the offences which you then laid to my charge. I have ever been a faithful wife to the king, though I do not say I have always shown him that humility which his goodness to me and the honour to which he raised me merited. I confess I have had jealous fancies and suspicions of him which I had not discretion and wisdom enough to conceal at all times.

But God knows, and is my witness, that I never sinned against him in any other way. Think not I say this in the hope to prolong my life. God hath taught me how to die, and he will strengthen my faith. Think not that I am so bewildered in my mind as not to lay the honour of my chastity to heart now in mine extremity, when I have maintained it all my life long, as much as ever queen did. I know these my last words will avail me nothing, but for the justification of my chastity and my honour.

As for my brother and those others who are unjustly condemned, I would willingly suffer many deaths to deliver them; but since I see it so pleases the king, I shall willingly accompany them in death, with this assurance, that I shall lead an endless life with them in peace.

AT THE SCAFFOLD

Good Christian people, I am come hither to die, according to law, for by the law I am judged to die, and therefore I will speak nothing against it.

I come here only to die. . . and thus yield myself humbly unto the will of my lord the King. I pray God to save the King and send him long to reign over you, for a gentler or more merciful Prince was there never. To me he was ever a good and gently sovereign lord.

If and person will meddle with my cause, I require them to judge the best. Thus I take my leave of the world and of you, and heartily desire you all to pray for me.

Anne then places her head on the block and repeated fearfully:

O Jesu, have mercy on my soul.
O Jesu have mercy on my soul.

POEMS WRITTEN BY ANNE BOLEYN

COMPOSED AFTER HER CONDEMNATION

Oh, death, rock me asleep,
Bring on my quiet rest,
Let pass my very guiltless ghost
Out of my careful breast
Ring out the doleful knell,
Let its sound my death tell;
For I must die,
There is no remedy,
For now I die!

My pains who can express,
Alas! They are so strong!
My dolour will not suffer strength
My life for to prolong
Alone in prison strange!
I wail my destiny;
Woe worth this cruel hap, that I
Should taste this misery.

Farewell my pleasures past,
Welcome my present pain,
I feel my torments so increase
That life cannot remain.
Sound now the passing bell,
Rung is my doleful knell,
For its sound my death doth tell.
Death doth draw nigh,
Sound the knell dolefully,
For now I die!

Defiled is my name, full sore
Through cruel spite and false report
That I may say for evermore,
Farewell to joy, adieu comfort.

For wrongfully he judge of me;
Unto my fame a mortal wound,
Say what ye list, it may not be,
Ye seek for that shall not be found.

A Portuguese Eye-witness's account
of the execution

And being minded to say no more, she knelt down upon both knees, and one of her ladies covered her eyes with a bandage, and then they withdrew themselves some little space, and knelt down over against the scaffold, bewailing bitterly and shedding many tears. And thus, and without more to say or do, was her head struck off; she making no confession of her fault, but saying, 'O Lord God, have pity on my soul.'

THE BEHEADING OF ANNE BOLEYN

KATHARINE OF ARAGON

LETTER OF KATHARINE OF ARAGON TO HER FATHER,
KING FERDINAND II OF ARAGON
2 December 1505
(Translated from Spanish—after her marriage she only wrote
in English)

Most high and most puissant lord,

Hitherto I have not wished to let your highness know the affairs here, that I might not give you annoyance, and also thinking that they would improve; but it appears that the contrary is the case, and that each day my troubles increase; and all this on account of the Doctor de Puebla, to whom it has not sufficed that from the beginning he transacted a thousand falsities against the service of your highness, but now he has given me new trouble; and because I believe your highness will think I complain without reason, I desire to tell you all that has passed.

Your highness shall know, as I have often written to you, that since I came into England, I have not had a single *maravedi*, except a certain sum which was given me for food, and this such a sum that it did not suffice without my having many debts in London; and that which troubles me more is to see my servants and maidens so at a loss, and that they have not the wherewith to get clothes; and this I believe is all done by hand of the doctor, who, notwithstanding your highness has written, sending him word that he should have money from the king of England, my lord that their costs should be given them, yet, in order not to trouble him, will rather entrench upon and neglect the

62

service of your highness.

Now, my lord, a few days ago, Donna Elvira de Manuel asked my leave to go to Flanders to be cured of a complaint which has come into her eyes, so that she lost the sight of one of them; and there is a physician in Flanders who cured the *infanta* Donna Isabel of the same disease with which she is affected. She laboured to bring him here so as not to leave me, but could never succeed with him; and I, since if she were blind she could not serve me, durst not hinder her journey.

I begged the king of England, my lord, that until our Donna Elvira should return his highness would command that I should have, as a companion, an old English lady, or that he would take me to his court; and I imparted all this to the doctor, thinking to make of the rogue a true man; but it did not suffice me—because he not only drew me to court, in which I have some pleasure, because I had supplicated the king for an asylum, but he negotiated that the king should dismiss all my household, and take away my chamber-equipage, and send to place it in a house of his own, so that I should not in any way be mistress of it.

And all this does not weigh upon me, except that it concerns the service of your highness, doing the contrary of that which ought to be done. I entreat your highness that you will consider that I am your daughter, and that consent not that on account of the doctor I should have such trouble, but that you will command some ambassador to come here, who may be a true servant of your highness, and for no interest will cease to do that which pertains to your service.

And if in this your highness trusts me not, do you command some person to come here, who may inform you of the truth, and then you will have one who will better serve you. As for me, I have had so much pain and annoyance that I have lost my health in a great measure; so that for two months I have had severe tertian fevers, and this

63

will be the cause that I shall soon die. I supplicate your highness to pardon me that I presume to entreat you to do me so great favour as to command that this doctor may not remain; because he certainly does not fulfil the service of your highness, which he postpones to the service of the worst interest which can be. Our Lord guard the life and most royal estate of your highness, and ever increase it as I desire. From Richmond, the second of December.

My lord, I had forgotten to remind your highness how you know that it was agreed that you were to give, as a certain part of my dowry, the plate and jewels that I brought; and yet I am certain that the king of England, my lord, will not receive anything of plate nor of jewels which I have used; because he told me himself that he was indignant that they should say in his kingdom that he took away from me my ornaments. And as little may your highness expect that he will take them in account and will return them to me; because I am certain he will not do so, nor is any such thing customary here.

In likewise the jewels which I brought from thence [Spain] valued at a great sum. The king would not take them in the half of the value, because here all these things are esteemed much cheaper, and the king has so many jewels that he rather desires money than them. I write thus to your highness because I know that there will be great embarrassment if he will not receive them, except at less price. It appears to me that it would be better if your highness should take them for yourself, and should give to the king of England, my lord, his money. Your highness will see what would serve you best, and with this I shall be most content.

The humble servant of your highness, who kisses your hands.

LETTER FROM KATHARINE OF ARAGON TO HER HUSBAND, KING HENRY VIII

(16 September 1513 after the Battle of Flodden,)

Sir,

My Lord Howard hath sent me a letter open to your Grace, within one of mine, by the which you shall see at length the great Victory that our Lord hath sent your subjects in your absence; and for this cause there is no need herein to trouble your Grace with long writing, but, to my thinking, this battle hath been to your Grace and all your realm the greatest honour that could be, and more than you should win all the crown of France; thanked be God of it, and I am sure your Grace forgetteth not to do this, which shall be cause to send you many more such great victories, as I trust he shall do.

My husband, for hastiness, with Rougecross I could not send your Grace the piece of the King of Scots coat which John Glynn now brings. In this your Grace shall see how I keep my promise, sending you for your banners a king's coat. I thought to send himself unto you, but our Englishmens' hearts would not suffer it. It should have been better for him to have been in peace than have this reward. All that God sends is for the best.

My Lord of Surrey, my Henry, would fain know your pleasure in the burying of the King of Scots' body, for he has written to me so. With the next messenger your Grace's pleasure may be herein known. And with this I make an end, praying God to send you home shortly, for without this no joy here can be accomplished; and for the same I pray, and now go to Our Lady of Walsingham that I promised so long ago to see. At Woburn the 16th of September.

I send your Grace herein a bill found in a Scotsman's purse of such things as the French King sent to the said King of Scots to make war against you, beseeching you to send Mathew hither as soon as this messenger comes to bring me tidings from your Grace.

Your humble wife and true servant, Katharine.

LETTER OF KATHARINE OF ARAGON TO HER DAUGHTER, PRINCESS MARY
April 1534

Daughter, I heard such tidings today that I do perceive if it be true, the time is come that Almighty God will prove you; and I am very glad of it, for I trust He doth handle you with a good love. I beseech you agree of His pleasure with a merry heart; and be sure that, without fail, He will not suffer you to perish if you beware to offend Him. I pray you, good daughter, to offer yourself to Him. If any pangs come to you, shrive yourself; first make you clean; take heed of His commandments, and keep them as near as He will give you grace to do, for then you are sure armed. And if this lady (Anne Shelton) do come to you as it is spoken, if she do bring you a letter from the King, I am sure in the self same letter you shall be commanded what you shall do.

Answer with few words, obeying the King, your father, in everything, save only that you will not offend God and lose your own soul; and go no further with learning and disputation in the matter. And wheresoever, and in whatsoever company you shall come, observe the King's commandments. Speak you few words and meddle nothing. I will send you two books in Latin; the one shall be *De Vita Christi* with a declaration of the Gospels, and the other the *Epistles of St Jerome* that he did write to Paul and Eustochium, and in them I trust you shall see good things. And sometimes for your recreation use your virginals or lute if you have any.

But one thing I especially desire you, for the love that you do owe unto God and unto me, to keep your heart with a chaste mind, and your body from all ill and wanton company, not thinking or desiring any husband for Christ's passion; neither determine yourself to any manner of living till this troublesome time be past. For I dare make sure that you shall see a very good end, and better than you can desire. I would God, good daughter, that you did know with how good a heart I do write this letter unto you. I never did one with a better, for I perceive very well that God loveth you. I beseech Him of His goodness to continue it; and if it fortune that you shall have nobody with you of your acquaintance, I think it best you keep your keys yourself, for howsoever it is, so shall be done as shall please them.

And now you shall begin, and by likelihood I shall follow. I set not a rush by it; for when they have done the uttermost they can, than I am sure of the amendment. I pray you, recommend me unto my good lady of Salisbury, and pray her to have a good heart, for we never come to the kingdom of Heaven but by troubles.

Daughter, whatsoever you come, take no pain to send unto me, for if I may, I will send to you.

Your loving mother,

Katharine the Queen.

LETTER OF KATHARINE OF ARAGON TO THE IMPERIAL AMBASSADOR, EUSTACE CHAPUYS

1535

Mine especial friend,

You have greatly bound me with the pains that you have taken in speaking with the king my lord concerning the coming of my daughter unto me. The reward you shall trust to have of God; for (as you know) in me there is no power to gratify what you have done, but only with my goodwill. As touching the answer which has been made you, that his highness is contented to send her to some place nigh me, so as I do not see her, I pray you vouchsafe to give unto his highness mine effectual thanks for the goodness which he shows to his daughter and mine, and for the comfort that I have thereby received; as as to my seeing of her, you shall certify that, if she were within one mile of me, I would not see her. For the time permitteth not that I should go about sights, and be it that I would I could not, because I lack provision therefore.

Howbeit, you shall always say unto his highness that the thing which I desired was to send her where I am; being assured that a little comfort and mirth, which she should take with me, should undoubtedly be half a health to her. I have proved the like by experience, being diseased of the same infirmity, and know how much good it may do that I say. And, since I desired a thing so just and reasonable, and that so much touched the honour and conscience of the king my lord, I thought not it should have been denied me.

Let not, for my love, to do what you may that this may yet be done. Here have I, among others, heard that he had some suspicion of the surety of her. I cannot believe that a thing so far from reason should pass from the royal heart of his highness; neither can I think that he hath so little confidence in me. If any such matter chance to be communed of, I pray you say unto his highness that I am determined to die (without doubt) in this realm; and that I, from henceforth, offer mine own person for surety, to the intent that, if any such thing should be attempted, that then he do justice of me, as of the most evil woman that ever was born.

The residue I remit to your good wisdom and judgment as unto a trusty friend, to whom I pray God give health.

Katharine the Queen.

LETTER OF KATHARINE OF ARAGON TO HER HUSBAND, KING HENRY VIII

7 January 1536
(The last letter written to him on her deathbed)

My most dear lord, king and husband,
The hour of my death now drawing on, the tender love
I owe you forceth me, my case being such, to commend
myself to you, and to put you in remembrance with a few
words of the health and safeguard of your soul which you
ought to prefer before all worldly matters, and before the
care and pampering of your body, for the which you have
cast me into many calamities and yourself into many troubles. For my part, I pardon you everything, and I wish to
devoutly pray God that He will pardon you also. For the
rest, I commend unto you our daughter Mary, beseeching you to be a good father unto her, as I have heretofore
desired. I entreat you also, on behalf of my maids, to give
them marriage portions, which is not much, they being
but three. For all my other servants I solicit the wages due
them, and a year more, lest they be unprovided for. Lastly, I
make this vow, that mine eyes desire you above all things.
Katharine the Quene.

JANE SEYMOUR

KING HENRY TO JANE SEYMOUR
(Whilst Anne Boleyn was still his wife)

My dear Friend and Mistress, The bearer of these few lines
from thy entirely devoted servant will deliver into thy fair
hands a token of my true affection for thee, hoping you
will keep it forever in your sincere love for me. Advertis-
ing you that there is a ballad made lately of great derision
against us, which if it go much abroad and is seen by you,
I pray you to pay no manner of regard to it. I am not at
present informed who is the setter forth of this malignant
writing but if he is found he shall be straitly punished
for it. For the things ye lacked I have minded my lord
to supply them to you as soon as he can buy them. This
hoping shortly to receive you in these arms, I end for the
present.

Your own loving servant and sovereign

H. R.

Letter of Queen Jane Seymour to the Privy Council of England

12 October 1537

(After the birth of her son Prince Edward—12 days before her death of puerperal fever.)

Right trusty and well beloved, we greet you well, and for as much as by the inestimable goodness and grace of Almighty God, we be delivered and brought in childbed of a prince, conceived in most lawful matrimony between my lord the king's majesty and us, doubting not but that for the love and affection which you bear unto us and to the commonwealth of this realm, the knowledge thereof should be joyous and glad tidings unto you, we have thought good to certify you of the same. To the intent you might not only render unto God condign thanks and prayers for so great a benefit but also continually pray for the long continuance and preservation of the same here in this life to the honour of God, joy and pleasure of my lord the king and us, and the universal weal, quiet and tranquillity of this whole realm. Given under our signet at my lord's manor of Hampton Court the 12th day of October.

Jane the Quene

ANNE OF CLEVES

LETTER OF ANNE OF CLEVES TO HER HUSBAND, KING HENRY VIII

11 July 1540
(In response to Henry's request for an annulment)

Pleaseth your most excellent majesty to understand that, whereas, at sundry times heretofore, I have been informed and perceived by certain lords and others your grace's council, of the doubts and questions which have been moved and found in our marriage; and how hath petition thereupon been made to your highness by your nobles and commons, that the same might be examined and determined by the holy clergy of this realm; to testify to your highness by my writing, that which I have before promised by my word and will, that is to say, that the matter should be examined and determined by the said clergy; it may please your majesty to know that, though this case must needs be most hard and sorrowful unto me, for the great love which I bear to your most noble person, yet, having more regard to God and his truth than to any worldly affection, as it beseemed me, at the beginning, to submit me to such examination and determination of the said clergy, whom I have and do accept for judges competent in that behalf.

So now being ascertained how the same clergy hath therein given their judgment and sentence, I acknowledge myself hereby to accept and approve the same, wholly and entirely putting myself, for my state and condition, to your highness' goodness and pleasure; most humbly beseeching

your majesty that, though it be determined that the pretended matrimony between us is void and of none effect,
whereby I neither can nor will repute myself for your
grace's wife, considering this sentence (whereunto I stand)
and your majesty's clean and pure living with me, yet it
will please you to take me for one of your humble servants, and so determine of me, as I may sometimes have
the fruition of your most noble presence; which as I shall
esteem for a great benefit, so, my lords and others of your
majesty's council, now being with me, have put me in
comfort thereof; and that your highness will take me for
your sister; for the which I most humbly thank you accordingly.

Thus, most gracious prince, I beseech our Lord God to
send your majesty long life and good health, to God's glory, your own honour, and the wealth of this noble realm.

From Richmond, the 11th day of July, the 32nd year of
your majesty's most noble reign.

Your majesty's most humble sister and servant,
Anne the daughter of Cleves.

KATHRYN HOWARD

LETTER OF QUEEN KATHRYN HOWARD TO MASTER THOMAS CULPEPER (CHARGED AND EXECUTED FOR ADULTERY WITH THE QUEEN) FOUND IN HIS PRIVATE LETTER-BOX

Kathryn's last words were—'I die a Queen, but would rather die the wife of Culpeper.'

Master Culpeper,

I heartily recommend me unto you, praying you to send me word how that you do. It was showed me that you was sick, the which thing troubled me very much till such time that I hear from you praying you to send me word how that you do, for I never longed so much for a thing as I do to see you and to speak with you, the which I trust shall be shortly now. That which doth comfortly me very much when I think of it, and when I think again that you shall depart from me again it makes my heart die to think what fortune I have that I cannot be always in your company.

It my trust is always in you that you will be as you have promised me, and in that hope I trust upon still, praying you that you will come when my Lady Rochford is here for then I shall be best at leisure to be at your commandment, thanking you for that you have promised me to be so good unto that poor fellow my man which is one of the griefs that I do feel to depart from him for then I do know no one that I dare trust to send to you, and therefore I pray you take him to be with you that I may sometime hear from you one thing. I pray you to give me a horse for my man for I had much ado to get one and therefore I pray send me one by him and in so doing I am as I said afor, and thus I take my leave of you, trusting to see you shortly again and I would you was with me now that you might see what pain I take in writing to you.

Yours as long as life endures,

Katheryn.

One thing I had forgotten and that is to instruct my man to tarry here with me still for he says whatsomever you bid him he will do it.

LETTER OF QUEEN KATHRYN HOWARD TO THE KING APPEALING FOR HER LIFE (NOT KNOWING THAT HE KNEW ABOUT THOMAS CULPEPPER).

I, Your Grace's most sorrowful subject and most vile wretch in the world, not worthy to make any recommendation unto your most excellent Majesty, do only make my most humble submission and confession of my faults.

Whereas no cause of mercy is deserved on my part, yet of your most accustomed mercy extended unto all other men undeserverd, most humbly on my hands and knees I do desire one particle thereof to be extended unto me, although of all other creatures I am most unworthy to be called either your wife or your subject.

My sorrow I can by no writing express, nevertheless I trust your most benign nature will have some respect unto my youth, my ignorance, my frailness, my humble confession of my faults, and plain declaration of the same referring me wholly unto Your Grace's pity and mercy.

First, at the flattering and fair persuasions of Manox, being but a young girl, I suffered him a sundry times to handle and touch the secret parts of my body which neither become me with honesty to permit nor him to require.

Also, Francis Derehem, by many persuasions procurred me to his vicous purpose and obtained first to lie upon my bed with his doublet and hose and after within the bed and finally he lay with me naked, and used me in such sort as a man doth his wife many and sundry times, but how often I know not.

Our company ended almost a year before the King's Majesty was married to my Lady Anne of Cleves and continued not past one quarter of a year or a little above.

Now the whole truth being declared unto Your Majesty, I most humbly beseech you to consider the subtle persuasions of young men and the ignorance and frailness of young women.

I was so desirious to be taken unto Your Grace's favour, and so blinded by with the desire of worldly glory that I could not, nor had grace to consider how great a fault it was to conceal my former faults from Your Majesty, considering that I intended ever during my life to be faithful and true unto Your Majesty ever after.

Nevertheless, the sorrow of my offenses was ever before my eyes, considering the infinite goodness of Your Majesty toward me which was ever increasing and not diminishing.

Now, I refer the judgement of mine offenses with my life and death wholly unto your most benign and merciful grace, to be considered by no justice of Your Majesty's laws but only by your infinite goodness, pity, compassion and mercy—without which I acknowledge myself worthy of the most extreme punishment.

KATHERINE PARR

Letter of Katherine Parr to her husband, King Henry VIII

July 1544
(Whilst he was away at the Siege of Boulogne)

Although the distance of time and account of days neither is long nor many of your majesty's absence, yet the want of your presence, so much desired and beloved by me, maketh me that I cannot quietly pleasure in anything until I hear from your majesty. The time, therefore, seemeth to me very long, with a great desire to know how your highness hath done since your departing hence, whose prosperity and health I prefer and desire more than mine own. And whereas I know your majesty's absence is never without great need, yet love and affection compel me to desire your presence.

Again, the same zeal and affection force me to be best content with that which is your will and pleasure. Thus love maketh me in all things to set apart mine own convenience and pleasure, and to embrace most joyfully his will and pleasure whom I love. God, the knower of secrets, can judge these words not to be written only with ink, but most truly impressed on the heart. Much more I omit, lest it be thought I go about to praise myself, or crave a thank; which thing to do I mind nothing less, but a plain, simple relation of the love and zeal I bear your majesty, proceeding from the abundance of the heart. Wherein I must confess I desire no commendation, having such just occasion to do the same.

I make like account with your majesty as I do with God for his benefits and gifts heaped upon me daily, acknowledging myself a great debtor to him, not being able to recompense the least of his benefits; in which state I am certain and sure to die, yet I hope in His gracious acceptation of my goodwill. Even such confidence have I in your majesty's gentleness, knowing myself never to have done my duty as were requisite and meet for such a noble prince, at whose hands I have found and received so much love and goodness, that with words I cannot express it. Lest I should be too tedious to your majesty, I finish this my scribbled letter, committing you to the governance of the Lord with long and prosperous life here, and after this life to enjoy the kingdom of his elect.

From Greenwich, by your majesty's humble and obedient servant,

        Katharine the Queen.

LETTER OF QUEEN KATHERINE PARR TO THE PRIVY COUNCIL

25 July 1544

(Referring to the successful Siege of Boulogne)

Katharine the Queen.

Right trusty and well-beloved cousins, we greet you well. Letting you wit that having received your letters of the 23rd of this present, we have by the same had singular comfort, as well to perceive thereby the state of health my lord the king's majesty was in at that present, as also the good beginning of success of his grace's affairs there; for your joyful news whereof we give unto you our right hearty thanks. And forasmuch as, touching the other contents of your said letters, we have presently written at length unto my said lord, the king's majesty, we forbear to repeat the same unto you, not doubting but that his highness will communicate the same unto you accordingly. Given under our signet at my said lord the king's majesty's honour of Hampton Court, the 25th day of July, the 36th year of his majesty's most noble reign.

LETTER OF KATHERINE PARR TO HER STEPDAUGHTER, PRINCESS MARY
20 September 1544
(Written in thanks for a gift of a purse embroidered by Mary)

Although, most noble and dearest lady, there are many reasons that easily induce my writing to you at this time, yet nothing so greatly moves me thereto as my concern for your health; which, as I hope it is very good, so am I greatly desirous to be assured thereof.

Wherefore, I despatch to you this messenger, who will be (I judge) most acceptable to you, not only from his skill in music, in which you, I am well aware, take as much delight as myself, but also because, having long sojourned with me, he can give the most certain information of my whole estate and health. And, in truth, I have had it in mind before this to have made a journey to you and salute you in person; but all things do not correspond with my will. Now, however, I hope this winter, and that ere long, that, being nearer, we shall meet; than which, I assure you, nothing can be to me more agreeable, and more to my heart's desire.

Now since, as I have heard, the finishing touch (as far as the translation is concerned) is given by Mallet to Erasmus's work upon John, and nought now remains but that proper care and vigilance should be taken in revising, I entreat you to send over to me this very excellent and useful work, now amended by Mallet, or some of your people, that it may be committed to the press in due time; and farther, to signify whether you wish it to go forth to the world (most auspiciously) under your name, or as the production of an unknown writer. To which work you will, in my opinion, do a real injury, if you refuse to let it go down to posterity under the auspices of your own name, since you have undertaken so much labour in accurately translating it for the great good of the public, and would have undertaken still greater (as is well known) if the health of your body had permitted.

And, since all the world knows that you have toiled and laboured much in this business, I do not see why you should repudiate that praise which all men justly confer on you. However, I leave this whole matter to your discretion and, whatever resolution you may adopt, that will meet my fullest approbation.

For the purse, which you have sent me as a present, I return you great thanks. I pray God, the greatest and best of beings, that He deign to bless you uninterruptedly with true and unalloyed happiness. May you long fare well in him.

From Hanworth, 20th of September,

    Most devotedly and lovingly yours,

                Katharine the Queen.

A Selection of Original Letters

(Extracts from *Ellis' Original Letters*).

SIR HENRY ELLIS

QUEEN KATHERINE TO THOMAS WOLSEY, AUGUST 13TH, 1513
(Expressing affection for the King's person)

Maister Almoner I received bothe your lettres by Cop-
ynger and John Glyn, and I . . . .veray gladde to here soo
well the King passeth his daungerous passage, the Fran-
shem (Frenchmen) being present. I trust to God it shal
soo continue that ever the King shal hau (have the) best
on his enemyes with as grete honor as ever King had. Til
I sawe your letter I (was) trobled to here soon ere the
King was to the siege of Tyrwyn for thinconvenients (of)
his own personne; but now I thanke God ye make me
suer of the good hede that the (King) taketh of himself to
avoid almoner (all manner) daungiers. I pray you good M.
Almoner remember the King always thus to continue: for
with his lif and helthe ther is noo thing in the world that
shall com to hym amys by the grace of God, and without
that I can see nomaner good thing shal falle after it: and
being suer th . . . ye will not forget this, I wol saye heein
no more. But I pray you to write to me, and though ye
have no grete matiers, yit I pray you sende me worde. . .
.the chief that is to me from the Kings own self. Ye may
think whan I put yo (you to) this great labor that I forgete
the grete besinesse that ye have in hand, but if ye re . . . .
in what caas I am that is without any comfort or pleasour
onlesse I here from you . . . ye wol not blame me to desire
you (though it be a short letter) to let me kno . . . from you
tidings as often as may bee, as my trusting deserneth unto

you. From hens I have noo thing to write to you, but that ye bee not so besy the . . . .warre, as we bee here uncombred with it. I meane that touching myne own . . . . for going farther wher I shal not soo often her (hear) from the King: and al his subj (subjects) bee veray gladde, I thanke God, to bee besy with the Scotts, for thay take it for (a) passse tyme. My hert is veray good to it, and I am horrible besy with making standerds, banners, and bagies (badges). I pray God furst to send ther with you a good . . . .as I trust he shal doo, and with that every thing her shal goo veray well. . . . you to sende me worde wheder ye received the lettres that I sent unto you to t. . . . .of the King my fader, and what answer he gave you to it. And with this . . . . an ende. At Richemount the xiij. Day of August.

Katherina the Qwene

Maister Almoner

QUEEN KATHERINE OF ARAGON TO HER DAUGHTER THE PRINCESS MARY

Doughter

I pray you thinke not that any forgetfulness hathe caused me to kepe Charles so long here, and answered not to your good letter, in the whiche I percyve ye wold knowe howe I doo. I am in that caas that the long absence of the King and you troubleth me. My helthe is metely good: and I trust in God, he that sent me the last dothe it to the best, and woll shortly torne it to the first to come to good effecte. And in the meabe tyme I am veray glad to here from You, especially when they shewe me that ye be well amended. I pray God to continue it to his pleasour. As for your writing in Lattine I am glad that ye shall change frome me to Maister Federston, for that shall doo you moche good, to lerne by him to write right. But yet some tymes I wold be glad when ye doo write to Maister Federston of your own enditing when he hath rede it that I may see it. For it shalbe a grete comfort to me to see You kepe your Latten and fayer writing and all. And soo I pray You to recommaunde me to my Lady of Salisbury. At Oborne (Woburn) this Fryday night.

    Your Loving mother

        Katherine the Qwene

Letter of summons to the Lady Cobham to attend the Coronation of Queen Anne Boleyn

Henry R.   By the King

Right dere and welbeloved we grete you well. And foras-
moche as we be determined upon the fest of Pentecost
next commyng to kepe and do to be celebrate at Westmynster, with all due circumstances of honor, the Coronacion of our derest wif the Lady Anne our queen, as to
her astate and dignitie doth appertain; and have appointed
you amongs other, at the same tyme, to geve your attendance on horseback in suche place as your degree apper-
taineth; We therefor desire and pray you to put yourself
in suche aredines as ye may be personally at our manor
of Grenewich the Fryday next before the said feest, then
and ther to give your attendance upon said Quene from
thens to our Towre of London the same day, and on the
next day to ryde from the same our toure, thorough our
cite of London, unto our manor of Westmynster, and the
next day, Witsonday, to go unto our Monastery ther to the
said Coronacion, providing for yourself and your womwn
some faire white, or white gray palfries, or geldings, suche
as ye shall thinke most fytt to serve for that purpose.

And as concernying the apparel of your own palfrey, ye
shalbe furnished thereof by the Master of the Horsses with
our said derest wif the Quene ay any your repaire or sending hider for the same in every behalf, saving for your bitt
and your bosses. Trusting that for the lyveraies and order-
ing of your said women aswell in their apparel as in their

horses ye woll in suche wise provide for them as unto your honor and that Solempnite apperteineth. and your robes and lyveraies shalbe delivered at any tyme, when ye shal come or sende for the same by the Keper of our Great Wardrobe: not failing hereof as ye entende to do us pleasour. Yeven under Signet at our manor of Grenewich the xxviijth day of Aprill.

To our right dere and welbeloved
The Lady Cobham.

THOMAS CRANMER ARCHBISHOP OF CANTERBURY, TO MR. HAWKYNS THE AMBASSADOR AT THE EMPEROR'S COURT.

(Upon the divorce of Queen Katherine, and the Coronation of Queen Anne Boleyn, 1533)

In my most hartie wise I commende me unto you and even so woulde be right gladd to here of your welfare, &c. Thes be to advertise you that inasmoche as you nowe and then take some paynes in wrytng unto me, I would be lothe you shuld thynke your labour utterly lost and forgotten for lake of wrytng agayne; therefore and bycause I reken you be somedele desirous of such newis as hath byn here with us of late in the Kyngis Graces matters, I entend to enforme you a parte thereof according to the tenure and purporte usyd in that behalf.

Ande Fyrste as towchng the small determynacion and concludyng of the matter of devorse between my Lady Kateren and the Kyngs Grace, whiche said matter after the convocacion in that behalf hadde determined and aggreed according to the former consent of the universities, yt was thowght convenient by the kyng and his lernyd Councell that I shud repayre unto Dunstable, which ys within iiij. Myles unto Amptell, where the said Lady Kateren keepeth her howse, and there to call her before me, to here the fynall sentance in this said mateir. Notwithstandyng she would not att all obey thereunto, for whan she was by doctor Lee cited to appear by a daye, she utterly refused

96

the same, sayinge that inasmoche as her cause was before the Pope she would have none other judge; and therefore woulde not take me for her judge.

Nevertheless the viijth daye of Maye, accordyng to the said appoyntment, I came unto Dunstable, my Lorde of Lyncoln beyng assistane unto me, and my Lorde of Wynchester, Doctour Bell, Doctour Claybroke, Doctour Trygonnel, Doctour Hewis, Doctour Olyver, Doctour Brytten, Mr. Beddell, with diverse other lernyd in the Lawe beyng concellours in the Lawe for the Kings parte: and soo there at our commyng kepte a courte for the apperance of the said Lady Kateren, where were examyned certyn witnes whiche testified that she was lawfully cited and called to appere, whome for fawte of apperance was declared contumax; procedyng in the said cause agaynste her *in pœnam contumaciam* as the processe of the Lawe thereunto belongeth; whiche contynewed xv. dayes after our cummyng thither. And the morrow after Assension daye I gave sentance therin, howe that it was indispensable for the Pope to lycense any suche marieges.

This donne, and after our reiornyng (returning) home agayne, the Kings Highness prepared al things convenient for the Coronacion of the Queene, whiche also was after suche a maner as foloweth.

The Thursdaye nexte before the feaste of Pentecost, the Kyng and the Queene beyng at Grenewyche, all the Craftes of London thereunto well appointed, in several bargis deckyd after the most gorgiouse and sumptuous maner, with dyverse pagiantes thereunto belongyng, repayred and wayted all together upon the Mayre of London; and so, well furnysshed, cam all unto Grenewiche, where they taryed and wayted for the Queenes commyng to her barge: which so done, they brought her into the Tower, trompetts, shambes, (shaums), and other dyverse instrumentes all the wayes playng and makyng greate melodie, which, as ys reported, was as combly donne as never was lyke in any tyme nyghe to our remembrance. And so her Grace cam to the Tower on Thursday at nyghte, abowte v. of the clocke, where also was such a pele of gonnes as hath not byn harde lyke a great while before. And the same nyghte, and Frydaye aldaye, (all day) the Kyng and Queene teryed there; and on Fridaye at nyght the Kyngs Grace made xviij knights of the Bathe, whose creacion was not alonly so strange to here of, as also their garmentes stranger to beholde or loke on; whiche said Knightes, the nexte daye, whiche was Saturday, rydde before the Queene's grace thorowte the Citie of London towards Westminster palice, over and besyds the moste parte of the nobles of the Realme, whiche lyke accompanied her grace thorowe owte the said citie; she syttyng in her here, upon a horse lytter, rychely appareled, and iiij knyghtes of the v. ports beryng a canapye over her hedd. And after her cam iiij.

Other furnysshed with diverse auncient old lades; and after them cam a great trayne of other ladies and gyntillwomen: whyche said progresse, from the begynnyng to thendyng, extended half a myle in leyngth by estimacion or thereaboute. To whome also, as she came alongeste the Citie, was shrewd many costely pagiants, with diverse other encomyes spoken of children to her; wyne also runyng at certeyne condits plenteously. And so procedyng throwte the streets, passid further unto Westminster Hall, where was a certyn blanket prepared for her, which donne, she was conveyd owte of the bake syde of the palice into a barge and unto Yorke Place, where the Kyng's grace was before her comyng, for this you muste ever presuppose that his Grace came allwayes before her secretlye in a barge aswell frome Grenewyche to the Tower as from the Tower to Yorke place.

Nowe than on Soundaye was the Coronacion, which also was of such a maner.

In the mornynge ther assembled withe me at Westminster

Churche the Bishop of London, the Bishop of Wynchester, the Bishop of Lyncoln, the Bishop of Dathe, and the
Bishop, and the Bishop of Saint Asse, the Abbote of Westminstre with x or xij moo Abbottes, whiche all revestred
ourselfs in our pontificalibus, and, soo furnysshed, with
our crosses and crossiers, procedid oute of the Abbey in a
procession unto Westminstre Hall, where we recyved the
Queene appareled in a robe of purple velvet, and all the
ladyes and gentillwomen in robes and gownes of scarlet
accordyng to the maner used before tyme in such besynes:
and so her Grace sustayned of eche syde with ij byssshops,
the Bysshope of London ande the Bysshop of Wynchester,
came furthe in processyon unto the Churche of Westminster, she in her here, my Lord of Suffolke beryng before
herr the Crowne and ij other Lords beryng also before her
a ceptur and a white roddle, and so entered up into the
highe Alter, where diverse ceremoneys used about her, I
did sett the crowne on her hedde, and then was sung *Te
Deum*, &c.

And after that was song a solempne Masse, all which
while her grace satt crowned upon a scaffold whiche was
made between the Highe Alter and the qwyer in Westminstre Churche; which Masse and ceremoneyes donne
and fynysshed, all the assemble of noble men brought her
into Westminstre Hall agayne, where was kepte a great
solempne feaste all that daye; the good ordre therof were
to longe to wrytte at this tyme to you. But now Sir you
may not ymagyn that this Coronacion was before her
mariege, for she was married muche about saint Paules
daye last, as the condicion therof dothe well appere by
reason she ys nowe sumwhat bygg with chylde. Notwithstandyng yt hath byn reported thorowte a greate parte of
the realme that I maried her; whiche was plainly false, for
I myself knewe therof a fortenyght after yt was donne.
And many other thyngs be also reported of me, whiche
be mere lyes and tales.

Other newys have we none notable, but that one Fryth, whiche was in the Tower in pryson, was appoynted by the Kyngs grace to be examyned befor me, my Lorde of London, my Lorde of Wynchestre, my Lorde of Suffolke, my Lorde Channcelour, and my Lorde of Wylteshire, whose opynion was so notably erroniouse, that we culde not dyspache hym but was fayne to leve hym to the determynacion of his Ordinarye, whiche ys the Bishop of London. His said opynion ys of suche nature that he thoughte it nat necessary to be beleved as an article of our faythe, that ther ys the very corporall presence of Christe within the Oste and Sacremente of the Alter, and holdethe of this poynte muste after the opynion of Oecolampadious.

And suerly I myself sent for hym iij or iiij tymes to perswade hym to leve that his imaginacion, but for all that we could do therin he woulde not applye to any counsaile, nothwithstandyng nowe he ys at a fynall ende with all examinacions, for my Lorde of London hathe gyven sentance and delyverd hym to the secular power, where he looketh every daye to goo unto the fyer. And ther ys also condempned with hyn one Andrew a taylour of London for the self same opynion.

★★★★

And thus farr you well, from my manor of Croydon the xvij. Daye of June.

Edward Earl of Derby and Sir Henry Faryngton to King Henry VIII,

(With the examinations of certain persons upon slanderous reports against Queen Anne)

Pleas it your Highness to be advertysed, that wher Sir William Fitzwilliam knight, on your Counsullors and Tresorer of your moost honourable Howse, lately directed his several lettres unto us your humble subgetts and servants Edward Erle of derby and Henry Faryngton Knyght, wherby we percyve your graces pleasor is that a lewde and noghty priest inhabytyng in thise parties, who hathe of late reported and spoken befor and in the audyence of certyn persons sundry and diverse unfyttyng and sklaunderous words, aswell by your Highnes as by the Quenes grace, shud not only be attached and sent up to your Highnes, but also that we shud in the accomplishement of your said pleasor take the examynacions and saings of suche persons as were present and herd the same unfyttyng and sklanderous reports and sayngs of the said priest in the premisses; and the same to send in wrytyng to your Highnes subscribed with our hands.

We according to our bounden duties in the accomplishement of your graces pleasor, have called befor us suche persons whose names and desposicions herafter do ensue; and the same persons did examyn upon ther others at Ley in the Countie of Lancaster, the xth day of August in the xxvth yere of the reign of your noble Highnes, Sir Richard Hoghton, Sir Willm Leylond knights, and Thomas Howcroft your servants and other of the Consaill of me said Erle beyng present with us. And the said Sir Henry hath attached the said priest and send hym to your Highnes.

And Sir Richard Clerke vyker of Leegh deposit and saith that the xx day of July last past he rede a proclamacion at Crofton, in the howse of John Blackeston's, concernyng Lady Katharin Princess-dowager, whiche Sir Jamys Harrison priest hering the said proclamacion, said that Quene Katharyn was Quene, and that Nan Bullen shud not be Quene, nor the King to be no King but on his bering.

Also Sir John Haworthe priest examyned saith upon his othe that he herd the said Sir Jamys saye that Quene Katharyn shud ne Quene, and as for Nan Bullen who the devell made her Quene; and as for the King shud not be King but on his bering.

Also William Dalton squyer examyned, and sworn upon a boke, deposit and saith that after that on Sir Richard Clerke had redde the said proclamacion, he redde certyn articles in the said proclamacion to the said Sir Jamys with certyn persons ther being present; the said Sir Jamys said I will take non for Quene but Quene Katherin; who the devell made Nan Bullen that hoore Quene, for I will never take hir for Quene, and the King on his bering: and then the said William said hold thy peace thou wots not what thou sais, and, but that thou art a priest, I shud punyshe the that other should take ensample.

John Dalton the elder, gentilman, sworn and examyned, saith that he was present when William Dalton squyer redde the said proclamacion, and the said Sir Jamys said I will call hir Quene Katharyn lettyng for noman, for Nan Bulleyn that noghty pake, (a female street-walker, a trull), or hoore, I do not remember whether, who the devell made hir Quene; and the King shalbe no King but on his bering.

Thomas Lathom the yonger, sworn and examyned, deposit and saith that, after that, a nother tyme, the same day and yere above said that Sir Jamys Harrison said that Nan Bullen that hoore shall not be Quene.

Jamys Woddes, sworn and examyned, deposit and saithe that he herd the proclamacion redde in the howse of John Blackston's and the said Sir Jamys said then that he wold not take non for the Quene but Quene Katharin; and as for Nan Bulleyn that hoore shalbe no Quene.

Adam Banaster, sworn and examyned, deposit and saith that Sir jamys Harrisin the xxiiij day of July in the howse of Thomas Grauesyns said that he wold never take Nan Bulleyn for Quene, to be hanged for the same, but for Nan Bulleyn.

Richard Sumner and John Clayton, sworn and examyned, deposen and say that they came in cumpenny with the said Sir James Harrison from the town of Perbalt to Eccleston, where the said Sir Jamys said unto theym this is a mervelous world, the King will put down the order of Priests and distroye the Sacrement, but will be as Thomas Dykonson said, that it cannot reign longe, for he saithe that Yorke wilbe London hastelye.

By Your humblyst and obedient servants

      E. Derby

      Henr. Faryngten Kt.

The six letters presented on the following pages relate to the arrest and behaviour in prison of Anne Boleyn. They are in part mutilated by the ravages of the 1731 Westminster fire, but are thought to still be of interest for the reader. Of Anne Boleyn's conviction we know nothing, the judicial documents relating to her trial are stated to have perished: but whether destroyed by Henry VIII or Elizabeth is not known.

Sir William Kingston to Secretary Cromwell, upon Queen Anne's committal to the Tower.

THYS ys to advertyse you apon my Lord of Nor-
folk and the Kyngs Counsell depart . . . from the
Towre I went before the Quene in to hyr lodgyng,
& . . .ᵃ sayd unto me M. Kyngston shall I go in
to adungyn. Now Madam y . .ᵇ shall go into
your logyng that you lay in at your Coronacion. It
ys to gu . .ᶜ for me, she sayd, Jesu have mercy on
me: and kneled downe wepyng a . . . . . pace, and
in the same sorow fell in to agret lawyng, and she
hathe done . .ᵈ mony tymes syns. And then she
desyred me to move the Kyngs Hynes that she . .
.ᵉ have the sacarment in the closet by hyr chambr,
that she my . . . . . for mercy, for I am as clere
from the company of man, as for s . . . .
. . am clere from you, and am the Kyngs trew
wedded wyf; and then sh . . . . . . M. Kyngston do you know wher for I am here, and I sayd nay,
and then . . . . . when saw you the Kyng and
I sayd I saw hym not syns I saw . . . . . . the
Tylte yerde and then M. K. I pray you to tell me
wher my . . . . fordᶠ ys, and I told hyr I saw
hym afore dyner in the cort. O. . . . . . my swet
brod'er. I sayd I left hym at York place, and so I
dyd I . . . . d she that I shuld be accused
with iij men and I can say . . . . . nay withyowt
I shuld oppen my body and ther with opynd . . .
. . . . res Hast thow accused me thow ar in the
towre with me, & . . . . I dy to gether
and marke thou art here to O my mother . . . . .
. . for sorow and meche lamented my lady of Wor-

cet' for by ca . . . . . · dyd not store in hyr body,
and my wyf sayd what shuld . . . .
sayd for the sorow she toke for me: and then she sayd
M. K . . . . . . with yowt just[a]; & I sayd the
porest sugett the Kyng . . . .
ther with she lawed. All thys sayings was yester ny
. . . . & thys moryng dyd talke with mestrys Cofy . . . . rea[a] dyd say on Sunday last unto the Quenes amn . . . . . . ere for
the Quene that she was a gud woman . . . . . .
. . Cofyn, Madam why shuld ther be hony seche
maters . . . . . . sayd she I bad hym do so for
I asked hym why he . . . . hys maryage
and he made ansur he wold tary . . . .
loke for ded mens showys, for yf owth can . . . .
. . . you wold loke to have mo; and he sayd yf he
. . . . he wold hys hed war of, and
then she sayd . . . . and ther with thay
fell yowt bot . . . . on Wysson monday
last . . . . . r that Nores cam mode u . . . .
. . . . age and further . . . .

. . . .

Wher I was commaunded to charge the gentelwemen
that y gyf thaye atende apon the Quene that ys to say
thay shuld have now commynycaseon with hyr in lese[b]
my wyf ware present, and so I dyd hit, notwithstaund-
yng it canot be: for my lady Bolen and mestrys Co-

---

[a] f. Norres. See Lord Herbert, p. 382.   [b] unles.

fyn lyes on the Quenes palet, and I and my wyf at the dore with yowt ro at* thay most nedes talke at* be without; bot I have every thyng told me by mestrys Cofyn that she thynks met for mee to knowe, and tother ij gentelwemen lyes with yowt me and as I may knowe . . . Kyngs plesur in the premysses I shall folow. From the Towre this mo . . . . . .

· S*r*. syns the makyng of thys letter the Quene spake of West[b] . . . . . . had spoke to hym by cause he dyd love hyr kynswoma . . . . he sayd he loved not hys wyf and he made anser to hyr . . . . . . loved won in hyr howse bettr then them bothe . . . . . . that it ys your self and then she defyed hym.

WILLM KYNG . . .

Sir William Kyngston to Secretary Cromwell, on Queen Anne's behaviour in Prison.

AFTER your departyng yesterday, Greneway gentilman ysshar cam to me, & . . . M. Caro and Mast' Bryan commanded hym in the Kyngs name to my . .[c] Ratchfort from my lady hys wyf, and the message was now more . . . . . se how he dyd; and also she wold humly sut unto the Kyngs Hy . . . .

. . for hyr husband; and so he gaf hyr thanks, and desyred me to know . . . . tyme he shuld cum affore the Kyngs counsell, for I thynk I s . . . . .

. cum forthe tyll I cum to my Jogement, wepyng very . . . . I departed from hym, and when I cam to the chambr the . . . . . . [a] of me and sent for me, and sayde I here say my lord my . . .

.[b] here; it ys trowth sayd I; I am very glad, sayd sh . . . . . . bothe be so ny together; and I showed hyr here wase . . . . Weston and Brerton, and she made very gud countenans . . . . I also sayd M. Page and Wyet wase mo, then she sayd he ha .

. . . on hys fyst tother day and ye here now bot ma . . . . . . I shall desyre you to bayre a Letter from me . . . . Secretory; and then I sayd madam tell it me by . . . . . . will do it, and so gaf me thanks saying I ha . . . . . .

that the Kyng's Counsell comes not to me and thys .

. . . . sayd we shuld have now rayne tyll she ware . . . . . . of the Towre. I pray you it may be-shortly by . . . . . . fayre wether. You know what I mayne the Quen . . . . . nyght that the Kyng wyst what he dyd wh . . . . . . ij abowt hyr as my lady Boleyn and Mestres . . . . Thay cowd tell hyr now thyng of my . . . . . .

. . nothyng ellys bot she defyed them all b . . . .

. . . . . sayd to hyr seche desyre as you heve ha

[a] f. Quene heard of me.   [b] f. brother la.

108

. . . . hase browthe you to thys and then
sayd . . . . ys the worst cheryssbe of
heny m . . . . wayres yernes she
sayd that was . . . . gentelman bot
he wase never in m . . . . ther
she sent for hym to ple . . . .
. . . logyng was . . . .
. . . .
. . . . for I
never spake with hym syns, bot apon Saterday before
May day, and then I fond hym standyng in the ronde
wyndo in my Chambr of presens, and 1 asked why
he wase so sad and he ansured and sayd it was now
mater, and then she sayd you may not loke to have ·
me speke to you as I shuld do to anobull man by cause
you be aninferer persson. No no Madam aloke sufficed me; and thus far you well . . he hathe asked
my wyf whether heny body maks thayr bed . . .
. . y wyf ansured and sayd nay I warant you, then
she say . . . . y myght make baletts Well
now bot ther ys non bet . . . . d that
can do it, yese sayd my wyf master Wyett by . . .
sayed trew.

. . . . my lord my brod' will dy.

. . . . ne I am sur thys was as WILLM KYNGSTON.

. . . tt downe to den' thys day.

. . . . thys day at diner I sent M. Nores hys
diner & sent hym . . . . aknave to hys

109

prest that wayted apon hym withe . . . .
. . . . t unto hym and he assured him agayn . . . .
. . . . ny thyng of my confession he
ys worthye to have . . . . hyt I defy
hym; and also he desyreth to hav . . . .
. . If anowre yf it may be the Kyngs plesur .

WILLM KYNG . . .

Sir William Kyngston to Secretary Cromwell, with further details of the Queen's conduct.

Sᵣ the Quene hathe meche desyred to have here in
the closet the sacarments, & also hyr Amner who she
supposeth to be Devet; for won owre she ys determyn-
ed to dy, and the next owre meche contrary to that.
Yesterday after your departyng I sent for my wyf, &
also for mestrys Coffyn to know how the* had done that
day, thay sayd she had bene very mery and made agret
dyner, and yet sone after she called for hyr supper,
havyng marvell wher I was all day; and after supper
she sent for me, and at my commyng she sayd " Wher
have you bene all day," and I mad ansure I had bene
with prysoners, " so" she sayd " I thowth I hard M.
tresur . . ." I ansured he was not here; then she be
gan talke and sayd I was crevely handeled . . . .
agreweche with the Kyngs Counsell with my lord of

* they.

110

Norfolke that he sayd . . . . . and shakyng hyr
hed iij or iiij tymes, and as for Master Tresurer he
was in the T . . . . . You know what she meynes
by that, and named M^r. Controler to be avery go . .
. . . . . she to be a Quene and crevely handeled
as was never sene; bot I . . . . dose it
to prove me, and dyd lawth with all and was very mery
and th . . . . ists and then I sayde
have now dowt ther . . . then she sayd yf hony
man . . . . ay & thay can bring now
wytnes, and she had talked with the gentell . . . .
. . . . sayd I knew at Marks commyng to the Towre
that nyght I reysayved . . . . . . at it was x. of
the cloke or he ware well loged and then she sayd . .
. . knew of Nores goyng to the towre and then
she sayd I had . . . . next yf it had bene
leyd she had wone, and then she sayd I w . . . . .
. . y bysshoppys for thay wold all go to the Kyng
for me for I thy . . . . . . Yngland prays for
me and yf I dy you shall se the grette . . . . . . e
withyn thys vij yere that ever cam to Yngland, & then
sh . . . . I have done mony gud dedys in
my days bot zit I thynke . . . . Kyng
to put seche abowt me as I never loved: I showed
. . . . . . to be honest and gud wemen bot I wold
have had . . . . br weche I favor most &c
WILLM KYNGST . .

To Mast^r. Secretary.

111

Edward Baynton to the Treasurer : declaring that only one person named Mark, will confess any thing against Queen Anne.

Mr THESAURER this shalbe to advertyse yow that here is myche communycacion that noman will confesse any thyng agaynst her, but allonly Marke of any actuell thynge. Wherfore (in my folishe conceyte) it shulde myche toche the Kings hono' if it shulde no farther appeere. And I cannot beleve but that the other two bee as f . . . culpapull as ever was hee. And I thynke assur . . . . the on kepith the others councell. As many . . . . conjectures in my mynde causeth me to thynk . . . specially of the communycacion that was last bet . . . the Quene and Master Norres. M. Aumener . . . me as I wolde I myght speke with M^r S . . . . . and yow together more playnely expresse my . . . yf case be that they have confessyd like wret . . . all thyngs as they shulde do than my n . . . . . . at apoynte. I have mewsed myche at . . . . . . of mastres Margery whiche hath used her . . . . strangely toward me of late being her fry . . .^a as I have ben. But no dowte it cann . . . . but that

^a *f.* fryad.

she must be of councell therewith . . . . hath ben great fryndeship betwene the Q . . . . . her of late. I herefarther that the Que . . standith styfly in her opynyon that she wo . . . . . . whiche I thynke is in the trust that she . . . . ther two. But if yor busynes be suche . . . . . . not com I wolde gladly com and wayte . . . . ke it requysyte. From Grenewy . . . . mornyng.

EDWARD . . . . . .

112

SIR WILLIAM KINGSTON TO SECRETARY CROMWELL, MAY 16TH 1536.

(Upon the preparations for the execution of Lord Rochford and Queen Anne)

Sir

Thys day I was with the Kyng's Grace and declared the petysyons of my Lord of Rochford wherin I was answrd. Sir the sayd Lord meche desyreth to speke with you, weche towchet hys consyens meche *as he sayth,* wherin I pray you I may know your pleasur, for by cause of my promysse made unto my sayd Lord to do the same, and also I shall desire you further to know the Kyngs plesur towchyng the Quene, as well for her comfyt as for the preparacion of skefolds and hother necessarys consernyng. The Kyngs grace showed me that my lord of Cantorbury shud be hyr confessar, and was here thys day with the Quene; and note in that mater, Sir, the tyme ys short, for the Kyng supposeth the gentleman to dy to morow, and my lord of Rocheford with the reysydew of gentleman, and as zit with yowt confession weche I loke for, bot I have told my lord of Rocheford that he be in aredynes to morrow to suffur execusyon, and so he accepse (accepts) it very well, and will do his best to be redy, notwithstanding he wold have resayved hys rights, weche hathe not bene used and in especiall here.

Sir I shall desyre you at (that) we here may prepayre for the same weche (*i.e.* what) ys necessary, for the same we here have now may for to do execusyon. Sir I pray you have gud rymembrance in all thys for hus (us) to do, for we shalbe redy al ways to our knowledge. Zit thys day at dyner the Quene sayd at (that) she shud go to Anvures (Anvers, Antwerp) and ys in hope of lyf, and thus far you well.

Willm Kyngston

EDWARD EARL OF HERTFORD, AFTERWARDS PROTECTOR TO LORD CROMWELL

(Upon the Kings intended marriage with Anne of Cleves)

Mi veri good Lord, after mi right harte commendacions, this schal be to advertise the name that this day the xiith of Juli, I reseyvid your letter dated att Okyng the ixth of the same, wher I perseyve your Lordship hath made me participant to the kyngs Highnes letters latli com from Master Wottun and the biship of Heriford, for which your jentell rememberans i most harteli thank your good lordship, and am as glad of the good resolution of the Deuk of cleeves his mother and Cunsell, as ever I was of thing sithen the birth of the Prense; for I think the kyngs Highnes should not in Christendum mari in no plas, might for his Grasis onar that should be lesse prejudiciall to his majestes succecion. And as conserning the other part of your letter, that the French Kyng begenith to be veri jentell to the Kyngs Highnes, I am right glad ther of, for that I think the amite of Aquamort will not long indeur, but I would aben (have been) more gladar yf that his jentillnis had prosedid of love and not for his porpos.

I am nothing sori to perseyve your lordship is lik schorteli to prove a profit (prophet), in that you would allweis sey yeu were suar the amite between the Emperour and French Kyng wouldnot continue: and as for your lordshipis rememberans of Shen I doo not dowght but that you woull accomplich hit when oportunite will sarve. I intend with Gods leve to se the Kyngs Highnes and your

Lordship with in a wik (week), wherfor I will forber fro fardar trubeling you att this time. Thus I comit you to God, hoo (who) send your lordship as well to far (fare) as I would mi sellfe. Fro Wollfall the xvij Juli with the ill hand of your lordshepis assured.

E. Hertford

(An eye-witness describing the execution of Queen
Kathryn Howard).

               At London the 15th day in February 1541
From Calleis I have harde nothing as yet of your sute to
my Lord Gray: and for news from hens, know ye, that
even according to my writing on Sonday last, I se the
Quene and the Lady Retcheford suffer within the Tower,
the day following (February 15th, 1542), whose sowles (I
doubt not) be with God, for thay made the moost godly
and chrystyan's end, that ever was hard to tell of (I thinke)
sins the worlds creation; uttering thayer lively faeth in the
blode of Christe onely, and with goodly words and stedfast
countenances thay desired all christen people to take regard unto thayer worthy and just punishment with death
for thayer offences, and agenst God hainiously from thayer
youth upward, in breaking all his commandements, and
also agenst the King's royall Majesty very daungeriously:
wherfor thay being justly condemned (as thay sayed) by
the Lawes of the Realme and Parlement, to dye, required
the people (I say) to take example at them, for amendment of thayer ungodly lyves, and gladly to obey the King
in all things, for whos preservation thay did hartely prey;
and willed all people so to do: commending thayer sowles
to God, and earnestly calling for mercy upon him: whom
I besieche to geve us grace, with suche faeth, hope, and
charite at our departing owt of this miserable world, to

come to the fruition of his god-hed in joy everlasting.
Amen

    Your loving brother

                  Otwell Johnson

With my harty commendacions unto Mr. Cave and Mistress Cave, not forgetting my syster your wiff, I pray you let them be made partakers of this last newes, for surely the thing is well worth the knowledge.

Fragment of a Letter of King Henry the Eighth to Queen Catherine Parr.

*** What remains of this Letter, is, itself, but a burnt fragment; the Volume containing it having been injured very much in the fire at Westminster in 1731. The portion here selected, is that part only which is written entirely in the King's hand. The early part of the Letter is in the hand of a Secretary. It was written before Boulogne, Sept. 8ᵗʰ. 1544.

. . . the closyng upp off thes our Letters thi . . . .
the castell affore namyd with the Dike is att our com-
. . . ment* and nott lyke to be recovert by the frence
men agayne, as we trust: not dwghtyng[b] with Gods
grace but that the castell and towne shall sortly[c] folow
the same trade: for as thys day, whyche is the viij[th]
day of September, we begynne thre bateryse, and
have iij. mynys goyng, by syd won whyche hath done
hys execution in scakyng[d] and teryng off woon off
theyre grettest bulwarkes.   No more to yow att thys
tyme swethart bothe for lacke off tyme and grett oc-
cupation off bysynes, savyng we pray yow to gyff in
our name our harte blessyngs to all our chyldren, and
recommendations to our cousin Margett[e] and the rest
off the lads[f] and gentyll women, and to our Consell
allsoo.   Wryttyn with the hand off your lovyng hows-
bande

HENRY R.

ᵃ commandment.   ᵇ doubting.   ᶜ shortly. -   ᵈ shaking.
ᵉ The Lady Margaret Douglas, who was niece to King Henry, may possibly be here meant.
ᶠ ladies.

119

LEONAUR

ALSO FROM LEONAUR
AVAILABLE IN SOFTCOVER OR HARDCOVER WITH DUST JACKET

THE WOMAN IN BATTLE by Loreta Janeta Velazquez—Soldier, Spy and Secret Service Agent for the Confederacy During the American Civil War.

BOOTS AND SADDLES by Elizabeth B. Custer—The experiences of General Custer's Wife on the Western Plains.

FANNIE BEERS' CIVIL WAR by Fannie A. Beers—A Confederate Lady's Experiences of Nursing During the Campaigns & Battles of the American Civil War.

LADY SALE'S AFGHANISTAN by Florentia Sale—An Indomitable Victorian Lady's Account of the Retreat from Kabul During the First Afghan War.

THE TWO WARS OF MRS DUBERLY by Frances Isabella Duberly—An Intrepid Victorian Lady's Experience of the Crimea and Indian Mutiny.

THE REBELLIOUS DUCHESS by Paul F. S. Dermoncourt—The Adventures of the Duchess of Berri and Her Attempt to Overthrow French Monarchy.

LADIES OF WATERLOO by Charlotte A. Eaton, Magdalene de Lancey & Juana Smith—The Experiences of Three Women During the Campaign of 1815: Waterloo Days by Charlotte A. Eaton, A Week at Waterloo by Magdalene de Lancey & Juana's Story by Juana Smith.

NURSE AND SPY IN THE UNION ARMY by Sarah Emma Evelyn Edmonds—During the American Civil War

WIFE NO. 19 by Ann Eliza Young—The Life & Ordeals of a Mormon Woman During the 19th Century

DIARY OF A NURSE IN SOUTH AFRICA by Alice Bron—With the Dutch-Belgian Red Cross During the Boer War

MARIE ANTOINETTE AND THE DOWNFALL OF ROYALTY by Imbert de Saint-Amand—The Queen of France and the French Revolution

THE MEMSAHIB & THE MUTINY by R. M. Coopland—An English lady's ordeals in Gwalior and Agra duringthe Indian Mutiny 1857

MY CAPTIVITY AMONG THE SIOUX INDIANS by Fanny Kelly—The ordeal of a pioneer woman crossing the Western Plains in 1864

WITH MAXIMILIAN IN MEXICO by Sara Yorke Stevenson—A Lady's experience of the French Adventure

LEONAUR

ALSO FROM LEONAUR
AVAILABLE IN SOFTCOVER OR HARDCOVER WITH DUST JACKET

A DIARY FROM DIXIE by Mary Boykin Chesnut—A Lady's Account of the Confederacy During the American Civil War

FOLLOWING THE DRUM by Teresa Griffin Vielé—A U. S. Infantry Officer's Wife on the Texas frontier in the Early 1850's

FOLLOWING THE GUIDON by Elizabeth B. Custer—The Experiences of General Custer's Wife with the U. S. 7th Cavalry.

LADIES OF LUCKNOW by G. Harris & Adelaide Case—The Experiences of Two British Women During the Indian Mutiny 1857. A Lady's Diary of the Siege of Lucknow by G. Harris, Day by Day at Lucknow by Adelaide Case

MARIE-LOUISE AND THE INVASION OF 1814 by Imbert de Saint-Amand—The Empress and the Fall of the First Empire

SAPPER DOROTHY by Dorothy Lawrence—The only English Woman Soldier in the Royal Engineers 51st Division, 79th Tunnelling Co. during the First World War

ARMY LETTERS FROM AN OFFICER'S WIFE 1871-1888 by Frances M. A. Roe—Experiences On the Western Frontier With the United States Army

NAPOLEON'S LETTERS TO JOSEPHINE by Henry Foljambe Hall—Correspondence of War, Politics, Family and Love 1796-1814

MEMOIRS OF SARAH DUCHESS OF MARLBOROUGH, AND OF THE COURT OF QUEEN ANNE VOLUME 1 by A. T. Thomson

MEMOIRS OF SARAH DUCHESS OF MARLBOROUGH, AND OF THE COURT OF QUEEN ANNE VOLUME 2 by A. T. Thomson

MARY PORTER GAMEWELL AND THE SIEGE OF PEKING by A. H. Tuttle—An American Lady's Experiences of the Boxer Uprising, China 1900

VANISHING ARIZONA by Martha Summerhayes—A young wife of an officer of the U.S. 8th Infantry in Apacheria during the 1870's

THE RIFLEMAN'S WIFE by Mrs. Fitz Maurice—The Experiences of an Officer's Wife and Chronicles of the Old 95th During the Napoleonic Wars

THE OATMAN GIRLS by Royal B. Stratton—The Capture & Captivity of Two Young American Women in the 1850's by the Apache Indians

LEONAUR

ALSO FROM LEONAUR
AVAILABLE IN SOFTCOVER OR HARDCOVER WITH DUST JACKET

PLAINS WOMEN *by Lydia Spencer Lane & Lodisa Frizzell*—Two accounts of American Women on the Western Frontier. I Married a Soldier or Old Days in the Old Army by Lydia Spencer Lane, Across the Plains to California in 1852 Journal of Mrs. Lodisa Frizzell by Lodisa Frizzell

THE WHITE SLAVE MARKET*by Mrs. Archibald Mackirdy (Olive Christian Malvery) and William Nicholas Willis*—An Overview of the Traffic in Young Women at the Turn of the Nineteenth and Early Twentieth Centuries

"TELL IT ALL" *by Fanny Stenhouse*—The Ordeals of a Woman Against Polygamy Within the Mormon Church During the 19th Century

TENTING ON THE PLAINS *by Elizabeth B. Custer*—The Experiences of General Custer's Wife in Kansas and Texas.

CAPTIVES! *by Cynthia Ann Parker, Mrs Jannette E. De Camp Sweet, Mary Schwandt, Mrs. Caroline Harris, Misses Frances and Almira Hall & Nancy McClure*—The Narratives of Seven Women Taken Prisoner by the Plains Indians of the American West

FRIENDS AND FOES IN THE TRANSKEI *by Helen M. Prichard*—A Victorian lady's experience of Southern Africa during the 1870's

NURSE EDITH CAVELL *by William Thomson Hill & Jacqueline Van Til*—Two accounts of a Notable British Nurse of the First World War. The Martyrdom of Nurse Cavell by William Thompson Hill, With Edith Cavell by Jacqueline Van Til.

AMERICAN FRONTIER WOMEN *by William W. Fowler*—The Exploits of Dozens of Pioneer Women of the United States.

FRANCES SLOCUM *by John F. Meginness*—The Story of a Quaker Girl's Abduction and Life among the Miami Indians.

MARGARET QUEEN OF SCOTLAND *by Henry Grey Graham*

PERSONAL RECOLLECTIONS OF JOAN OF ARC *by Mark Twain*

WITH THE IMPERIAL CAMEL CORPS IN THE GREAT WAR *by Geoffrey Inchbald*—The story of a serving officer with the British 2nd battalion against the Senussi and during the Palestine campaign.

CPSIA information can be obtained at www.ICGtesting.com
Printed in the USA
LVOW06*1120261213

366777LV00002B/119/P